A CHALLENGING TRANSITION IN SOMALIA

A STORY OF PERSONAL COURAGE
AND CONVICTION

A CHALLENGING TRANSITION IN SOMALIA

A STORY OF PERSONAL COURAGE
AND CONVICTION

Abdiweli Mohamed Ali

Institute for Peace and Security Studies

THE RED SEA PRESS
TRENTON | LONDON | NEW DELHI | CAPE TOWN | NAIROBI | ADDIS ABABA | ASMARA | IBADAN

THE RED SEA PRESS
541 West Ingham Avenue | Suite B
Trenton, New Jersey 08638

Book design: Dawid Kahts
Cover design: Ashraful Haque

Library of Congress Cataloging-in-Publication Data

Names: Ali, Abdiweli Mohamed, author.
Title: A challenging transition in Somalia : a story of personal courage and conviction / Dr. Abdiweli Mohamed Ali.
Description: Trenton : Red Sea Press, 2017. | Includes bibliographical references and index.
Identifiers: LCCN 2017003329| ISBN 9781569025154 (hb : alk. paper) | ISBN 9781569025161 (pb : alk. paper)
Subjects: LCSH: Ali, Abdiweli Mohamed. | Economists--Somalia--Biography. | Politicians--Somalia--Biography. | Somalia--Politics and government--1991-
Classification: LCC DT407.3.A47 A3 2017 | DDC 967.73053092--dc23
LC record available at https://lccn.loc.gov/2017003329

CONTENTS

ACKNOWLEDGEMENTS

I would like to dedicate this book to the men and women who have served Somalia and the country in its hour of need having risked life and limb in the process. A virtue exemplified best by my late friend and former Chief of Staff Abdishakur Mohamoud Elmi.

I would like to thank former President of Somalia Sheikh Sharif Ahmed for giving me the opportunity to serve my country. Exceptional thanks is reserved for former Prime Minister of Somalia Mohamed Abdullahi Farmajo for his efforts in enticing me to join his cabinet as a Minister of Planning and International Cooperation, appointing me as the Deputy Prime Minister of Somalia, and finally selecting me as his replacement as Premier.

Much of what has been achieved in the period, which this account will highlight, was made possible, thanks to earnest support and partnerships facilitated by the former Special Representative to Somalia Ambassador Augustine Mahiga and the leadership of Ban Ki-Moon. A special recognition is reserved for the men and women in the security forces who risked their lives daily to restore the peace, and of course, our comrades and friends in the African Union Mission for Somalia (AMISOM) and our international allies and partners. To my Council of Ministers thank you for your handwork and dedication.

I would be remiss to leave out Niagara University in my expressions of thanks. As a world-class institution, they offered me the opportunity to teach and support my family in Buffalo. They then extended me the courtesy of sabbatical leave to go out and fulfill my civic duty and help my country. I am gracious for the support and understanding this historic academic institution has provided for me.

My family deserves a special place in my thanks; they supported me throughout my tenure in politics and for this I am grateful. I would like to thank my wife for looking after my affairs and children. Few men get far without a crutch or support. I thank my family for being there when I needed them.

I would like to say a special thank you to the Institute for Peace and Security Studies at Addis Ababa University for the fellowship and support that made the book possible. Equally, thank you to the hard-working staff at the institute who supported me directly and indirectly. Mulugeta Gebrehiwot Berhe, Dr. Simon Akindes, Michelle Ndiaye Ntab deserve a special mention.

I am equally grateful to my Assistant Idil Abshir for her valuable input and for helping me transcribe the chapters of the book. Without her dedication, hard work, and diligence, this book would not have been possible. A heartfelt thank you to Dr. Lidwien Kapteijns for the valued notes and my Publisher Kassahun Checole and my Assistant and Technical Advisor Mohamed Abdullahi Mohamed for their efforts and careful work in helping me make the book complete.

Finally, I would like to express my heartfelt gratitude to the team in the Office of the Prime Minister who have made it possible to actualize the Roadmap process and implement my vision, in particular my Chief of Staffs Abdirahman Warsame Abdi (Burhan) and Abdishakur Mohamoud Elmi. Special thanks to my diligent and hardworking Policy Coordinator Sagal Abshir and my Special Assistant Hassan Awil Farah.

"If you are going to a desert, why not go to the one where you really belong?"

INTRODUCTION

Defining Somalia as my home is a bittersweet contradiction. For those that knew the world that existed before 1991 will remember, not the "world's most failed state" but, rather, a myriad of urban metropoles and rural oases, a place that encouraged education, empowered men and women to be the best that they could be.

Many people would accuse me of viewing the past with rose tinted glasses. But it was this past; this vision of what was and what could be that pushed me to return home. After a lifetime away, I landed in a warzone, determined that this was not all that we could be. I was compelled to leave a safe environment to come back.

In the short time that I sat at the helm of what would become the closing chapter of the Transitional Federal Government of Somalia I saw an opportunity to inspire change, to look beyond the rubble and destruction that lay around me and strive for something more. In this account I will demonstrate a little of what I discovered in the arenas of conflict resolution, policy formation, the inception and implementation of the National Roadmap for The End of Transition, the framework by which Somalia was to leave behind two decades of lawlessness, disorder, anarchy and chaos and chart a new era, based on the rule of law.

I am not so bold to suggest that I was alone in getting through my term in office. I was blessed to have people around me that shared my vision and dedicated their lives to seeing that vision come to fruition.

My staff in the Office of the Prime Minister worked tirelessly since June 2011 to achieve these goals, often forsaking their own safety. I was fortunate to have a cabinet of Ministers around me who adhered to their duty with sincerity and dedication.

The gravity of the situation and the scale of the task back in 2011 certainly was a guaranteed recipe for many a sleepless nights. The worst droughts to hit the region for nearly 60 years had deprived an already impoverished people, who were living under the onslaught of the radicalism espoused by the Al-Qaeda affiliated Al-Shabaab militants. A great number of people, at the time estimated to be well over 2 million were on the brink. Saving the lives of our countrymen was the first priority and port of call.

The relative success of the security forces in liberating the country from the extremists turned the tide and made it feasible for the first time in over two decades to entertain new opportunities and possibilities.

Somalia today has an interim constitution on which to build a progressive framework. The country has experienced elections being staged within the country's borders for the first time since 1967. The capital city is free from the reign of terror imposed by the thugs and enforcers of Al-Shabaab. Their last remaining major stronghold, Kismayo is now under the control of the government.

There is much to be hopeful about, and the newfound optimism amongst the Somali people is one built on solid foundations and the country now has a genuine hope for the future.

Dr. Abdiweli Mohamed Ali

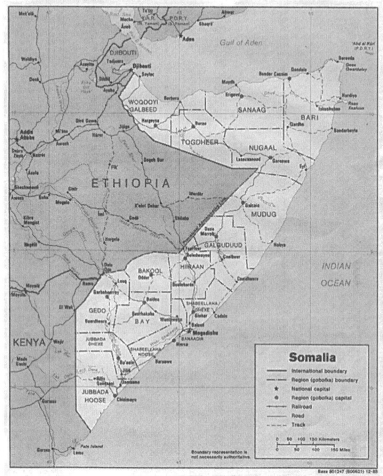

Map of Somalia

TIMELINE OF SIGNIFICANT EVENTS

- June 23, 2011: Appointed as Prime Minister
- June 28: Parliament approves nomination as Prime Minister
- July 23: Parliament Approves the Cabinet selection
- September 4-6: First Roadmap Conference
- December 15-17: Garowe I Conference
- February 15-17, 2012: Garowe II Conference
- February 23: London Conference
- March 29: Galkayo Agreement
- May 31-June 2: Istanbul Conference on Somalia
- August 1: National Constituents Assembly approves Interim Constitution
- August 20: Members of the new Parliament are sworn in
- August 28: Parliament votes to select the Speaker of the House
- September 10: Presidential elections culminate with the selection of President Hassan Sheikh Mahmoud
- October 6: President Hasssan Sheikh Mahmoud appoints Abdi Farah Shirdon as Prime Minister
- October 17 Parliament confirms Prime Minister Shirdon
- October18: Prime Minister Abdiweli Ali leaves office.

Dr. Abdiweli Mohamed Ali, Prime Minister of Somalia speaks at the Mini-Summit on Somalia September 23, 2011 United Nations New York UN Photo Eskinder Debebe

Dr. Abdiweli Mohamed Ali, Prime Minister of the Transitional Federal Government of the Somali Republic, addresses the general debate of the sixty-seventh session of the General Assembly September 27, 2012 United Nations, New York UN Photo/J Carrier

CHAPTER

1

BEGINNINGS:

GROWING UP IN SOMALIA

My Early Days

I was born to a nomadic family in 1960 or 1961, in the countryside of Galkayo, Somalia, in the area commonly known as "the Reserve Area." I was the third-born child in the family. Like many Somali nomads, my parents did not know the exact year of my birth; they estimated the year by using the celestial calendar of the nomadic society.

My mother, having only two brothers, belonged to a relatively small and close-knit family. My father was the eldest male in a large nomadic family, the Ali-Gaas family, and thus was looked upon to provide leadership. An outspoken personality, he was known for speaking truth to power. He was also a gentle giant and a kind father to his children.

My father found the life of a nomad unbearable and unforgiving. In 1965, when I was four or five years old, he decided to spare my older brother and I the nomadic life. He wanted us to have the opportunities afforded by a big city, so he sent us to Mogadishu to stay with his younger brother, Abdulkadir Ali-Gaas. Our departure to Mogadishu coincided with one of the severest droughts in Somalia. It was known as the baastaaley, or the spaghetti drought, because although the staple diet in Somalia's countryside was milk and meat, spaghetti was the most commonly donated food to drought-afflicted Somalis. So, because of the drought, we ate spaghetti.

Uncle Abdulkadir was making a good living at the time, working for an American company. He was earning $1,000 a month, and in the 1960s that was not small change. He was a driller, a good one, and not a bad mechanic either.

To this nomad boy, Mogadishu in the 1960s was a huge metropolis. All I knew at that early age was a life of goats and sheep, and I was amazed at everything I saw in Mogadishu. Perhaps the most amazing sight was also the most unexpected one: the Indian Ocean. I had never seen a large body of water before, let alone an ocean. Somalia's rural areas have access to only small pools of water, such as ponds and oases. When I saw this huge sea from a distance, the bubbles and foam on the ocean's blue surface resembled goats grazing on blue ground. I wondered, what is this blue thing with goats on it?

My cousin Dahir Hersi Tahlil took me under his wing and showed me around Mogadishu. We went to the Lido beach on my first day there. Dahir tried to convince me to swim in the ocean, but when I saw the roaring waves all I could do was watch and wonder. I asked Dahir incessantly about the baffling things I noticed in the big city: the size of the shops and the variety of the products they sold; the streetlights, which particularly in the evening looked like small stars that I could reach out and touch; and the multitude of vehicles in the city and the noise they made.

About two months after my brother and I arrived in Mogadishu, Uncle Abdulkadir decided he was not able to provide for both of us. This surprised everyone, given his high earnings and the small size of his family at that time. Nevertheless he decided to keep my older brother and send me back home. I would be returned to the countryside to help my father tend his camels.

I had mixed feelings about this. On the one hand, I was sad not to be able to stay in Mogadishu and attend school; on the other hand, I was going back to my father and mother and an environment I knew well. I had missed my home and was homesick. I didn't miss fetching water and herding camels, goats, and sheep, but I had missed the kindness and compassion of my mother. So, while I was disappointed, I was not distraught. Returning to my home was not a bad thing under the circumstances.

In those days, children were taken to the countryside after

school closings to learn more about Somali culture and to become proficient in the Somali language. Not long after Uncle Abdulkadir's decision, a distant aunt of mine in Mogadishu said she was going to visit the countryside with her family. My uncle said to her, "If you're going to Galkayo, you might as well take this young boy back to his father." There were no buses running then, so my aunt took me with her in a commodity truck from Mogadishu to Galkayo.

When we reached Dusamareb, about halfway between Mogadishu and Galkayo, the truck stopped at a gas station. My aunt pointed to a nearby house. "That's your uncle's house," she said. "Abdullahi Ali-Gaas and his family. He owns a shop that sells cigarettes and sugar. Why don't we go over and greet them while the truck is filling up with gas?" So we made our way over to the house.

When we entered the house, I did not recognize anyone there. One of the women, though, was my aunt Asha Ali-Gaas, my father's sister. When she saw me, she started to cry and was soon hugging and kissing me. In the midst of this emotional rollercoaster, my uncle returned home from his shop. Puzzled, he asked who I was. Aunt Asha cried, "This is your nephew! This is Hudi's son," referring to my father's nickname. (Hudi means very light color; my father was light-colored.) "And what is he doing here?" my uncle asked.

My story was told to everyone in the house. My uncle said to my distant aunt, "And you are taking him back to the countryside?" She replied that she was. What made the difference—what saved the day for me—was Aunt Asha's emotional state. Throughout the exchange, she kept kissing and hugging me, and she wasn't about to let me go. My uncle, having now heard my entire story, paused, looked at my distant aunt, and said: "You can go. Just leave him behind, leave him here. I will call Abdulkadir and let him know."

With those words, I was saved from the life of a nomad. I often wonder what would have happened if the truck had not stopped at the gas station to fill up—what would have happened if I hadn't had the opportunity to visit my uncle's house? What would have happened if Aunt Asha had not been there at the time? I might have gone back to the countryside and returned to the life of a nomad.

I was given a nice lunch, and in the afternoon I accompanied my uncle to his shop. He gave me some sage advice, together with a stern warning: "You can stay with me only if you go to school and learn the Qur'an. If you want to learn, you can stay. This house is only for people who want to learn and become useful. Otherwise, you might as well go back to herding camels. I am asking you now: Are you willing to go to school and learn the Qur'an?" I quickly replied: "Yes!"

To ensure that his point was not taken as an empty threat, my uncle told me that just a few days earlier he had sent the younger brother of his wife back to the unforgiving environment of the countryside. "I sent Mahmoud back," he said, "because he wasn't willing to go to school and improve himself. You're no different! He was my brother-in-law and my cousin, and I sent him back. So, my friend, if you're not willing to learn and go to school and work hard, you might as well go back to your father in the countryside."

I got the message quite clearly—if I wanted to stay with my uncle and aunt, nothing could take precedence over education.

I was fortunate that my uncle's wife, Halima Farah, was a kind woman with a gentle soul. She raised me as if I were her firstborn son, and I felt that she treated me better than she treated her own children. A couple of days after arriving in Dusamareb, I began studying the Qur'an under the tutelage of Moallim Mohamed Warsame. Moallim Mohamed was a kind-hearted and considerate teacher, pious and deeply spiritual. Two of his sons, Ahmed and Abdi, were fellow students at the same seminary, but he treated them no differently than he did the rest of us.

My Uncle Abdullahi too, despite his initial sternness, was a gentle and kind man. He was caring and compassionate, yet also serious and blunt; not very religious, but moderate in his words and actions. As he had told me, he placed a lot of importance in education and believed that it made all the difference in the world. He wanted his children and other relatives to study, to learn, and to succeed. Yet, strangely enough, though he could read and write the Somali script, he was not a learned man. He had begun working at a young age, in restaurants in Galkayo, first as a dishwasher, then as a busboy, and later as a waiter. Eventually, he saved enough money to start a modest business of his own.

My uncle's shop was known for selling two popular brands of

cigarettes, Rothmans and Craven, and the teachers who smoked these brands regularly stopped at his shop. Sometimes my uncle struck up conversations with the teachers to ask how I was progressing in school, and usually they would offer comments on my grades and exam performance. When my uncle returned home from the shop, often out of the blue he would say to me: "Yesterday I heard you had an English test. How did you do?" Of course, the teachers either had told or would tell him my grades, so I could not lie. There was no room for slacking off or playing around.

I stayed with my uncle and aunt in Dusamareb until graduating from high school in 1979. I do not think I disappointed them when it came to my studies, as I always came first or second in my class, succeeding both in school and in studying the Qur'an. Thanks to the kindness and generosity of my family and my stable and supportive home environment, my school performance surpassed everyone's expectations. I completed the Qur'an twice and became very proficient, nearly hafid—that is, I memorized nearly the whole Qur'an. Memorizing the Qur'an in those formative years was an excellent mental exercise that was a great help to me in my later school years. (Unfortunately, I have since forgotten most of it.) My school performance then was quite important not just to me, but to my extended family, as my younger cousins looked up to me. The expectation of my uncle and everyone else was that I would serve as a role model. I hope I did.

My uncle, for his part, continued to amaze me. After taking care of me, he continued to raise many relatives as well as other children with whom he had no blood or familial relations. All the children he took under his wings were the children of nomads. We can never repay our debt to him, and I am eternally grateful for all he did.

The 1960s: A Time of Optimism

From 1960 to 1969, under the government of Presidents Aden Abdulle Osman and Abdirashid Ali Sharmarke, Somalia enjoyed full-fledged democracy, with a respect for the rule of law and government transparency unprecedented in its time and in the region. Economically it was still a backward country, but it had all the necessary ingredients to allow it to move toward a thriving economy.

Clans in Somalia play a large role socially, politically, and economically. In Somali society, political representation is a complicated and often convoluted matter. It is usually related to notions of descent and the perceived power, size, and territorial control of clans. During the 1960s these clan narratives were openly expressed, but the conversations were generally non-toxic. Sporadic clan disputes arose, mostly over grazing land and water, but this animosity was not as visceral as it was to become in later years.

Also during this decade, Somalis enjoyed new freedoms. Civil liberties were extended to all citizens; elections were held for members of Parliament, and representatives from all the country's regions were elected in free and fair elections that in turn elected the head of state. Aden Abdulle Osman, the founding father of Somalia, and Abdirashid Ali Sharmarke, his first prime minister and later his political opponent, were elected through this process. These two men were the architects of a sound democratic system in Somalia. Both were members of the Somali Youth League (SYL), Somalia's dominant political party and the party that had led the nation to independence in 1960.

These two great patriots were not alone: Somalia during the 1960s had several other leaders who believed in and pushed for democracy at all levels. These leaders included Abdirizak Hagi Hussein and Abdullahi Isse Mohamud. Abdirizak, who served as Somalia's prime minister from 1964 to 1967 and was one of the most efficient administrators Somalia has produced, was known for his audacity in fighting corruption and malfeasance. Abdullahi Isse Mohamud, who had been Somalia's first prime minister under the Italian Trusteeship from 1956 to 1960, also served the newly independent state in various capacities after independence, from 1960 to 1969. Abdullahi took the helm in a very precarious and difficult period, leading Somalia during its fragile transition. He was widely considered fair and just, far removed from nepotism and clan influences.

Although there were isolated incidents of voting improprieties and rigged elections during this decade, usually the system worked smoothly. Somalis were able to organize freely in the political parties and other political groupings of their choice. More than eighty political parties were registered in the parliamentary elections of March 1969. There was a significant and powerful opposition, with a strong constituency and an even stronger possibility of winning elections.

The judicial system too was equitable and efficient. Justice was truly blind. Every Somali was equal under the law and had access to an independent, nondiscriminatory judiciary. Citizens were protected from political imprisonment and political exile. There was not a single Somali political prisoner during this democratic period.

The rule of law in a country should reflect the degree to which its citizens are willing to accept the institutions that make and implement laws and adjudicate disputes. The effectiveness of the rule of law in Somalia is clearly indicated in the following example. If someone assaulted you, all you had to do was report it to the police. The police would oblige you to go to the hospital, obtain an assessment of the injury, and then take that assessment to the court. The judge would issue a summons and set a court date. You would deliver the summons to your assailant, who had no choice but to appear in court. Failure to do so was a criminal offense. There was no need for police officers to show up at the perpetrator's doorstep to force him or her to appear in court. Somalis had such a high regard for the law.

The media, too, were free and independent. Some were very critical of the government, and others were outright supporters of the opposition political parties. Trade unions flourished, having strong bargaining powers on behalf of their members, as did many private businesses.

In stark contrast to the fundamentalist dogmas threatening Somalia today, a variety of religious institutions thrived in the country in the 1960s. Not only Islam but also Christianity was practiced openly. Mennonite missions were established in Jowhar and Jamame, and the Roman Catholic cathedral was a cultural landmark in Mogadishu. Somalis also enjoyed complete personal and social freedom of movement, choice of residence, and equality of opportunity. Although some corrupt practices occurred in the conduct of business affairs, government indifference was rare.

In addition to enjoying these comprehensive political freedoms and civil liberties, Somalis had the economic freedom to own and dispose of private property, to keep what they earned, and to exchange and trade goods and services without government interference. All this relative harmony ended with the election of 1969.

The Election of 1969: A Prelude to Dictatorship

Dusamareb, the capital of Galguduud, was an important battleground in the parliamentary elections of March 26, 1969. The city, in the center of Somalia, was diverse and multi-clan. The election there was marred by clan violence. Two main clans inhabited Dusamareb: the Ayr sub-clan of the Habar Gidir clan of the main Hawiye group and the Marehan clan of the Darod clan family.. There were also many members of the Majertein clan, originally from what is now Puntland State. My uncle was one of the Majertein members who had stumbled into Dusamareb, found it attractive, and settled there.

Dusamareb's three parliamentary seats were contested by more than a dozen political parties dominated by politicians from the Ayr and Marehan, sub-clans of clans that in turn allied themselves with other clans to gain power. There were also power struggles within the Ayr and Marehan. The law of unity and the struggle of opposites were perfected in this election.

The parliamentary candidates of the Somali Youth League (SYL) were favored to win, not through the popular vote, but through mechanisms that the SYL had put in place: determined to win at any cost and by any means necessary, the SYL ensured that the district authorities and election staff were dominated by SYL supporters. The three SYL candidates—Aden Shire Jama (Aden Low), Mahad Dirir Guled, and Mohamed Siad Barre—all of whom belonged to the Reer Dini sub-clan of the Marehan, were related through marriage, as they had married three sisters. Major General Siad Barre, the chief of the Somali armed forces, was not eligible to contest the election unless he resigned from his position, so he supported his cousin Ali Shire Warsame.

This was a hard-fought election, in which even relatives and in-laws were fair game. Nevertheless, despite political machinations and intrigues, it was open and transparent and Dusamareb buzzed with political activity. A variety of political parties, broadcasting creative slogans and featuring colorful candidates, occupied the political landscape. The parties had nightly assemblies, and the crowds were entertained with passionate speeches that were occasionally intertwined with music and traditional dances. I was a young boy at the time and, though not politically aware, I was enthralled by the songs, slogans, and dances.

What was so remarkable about the election of 1969 was the diversity of the parties' supporters. Every adult in our household belonged to and supported a different political party. Uncle Abdullahi was a big fan of Abdikassim Salah Hassan, the son of a prominent Ayr elder and a young university graduate from Russia. His wife, Halima Farah, supported Yassin Gelle Warsame, another graduate from Russia, who belonged to the Wagardha sub-clan of the Marehan. My cousin Noora Hirsi Tahlil was an ardent supporter of Mohamed Hirsi, a businessman and longtime resident of Oman. He belonged to the Reer Siyad Hussein sub-clan of the Marehan, while my cousin Abdikarim Mohamed Barre was a member of the youth group of another party with a parliamentary candidate belonging to the Sa'ad sub-clan of the Habargedir clan. Each member of the household voted for the candidate of his or her liking, and none of the candidates had any blood or clan relationship with these voters. They were voting from their conscience.

Nevertheless, after the election, a number of candidates were furious with the results. Since only one member of the SYL had received enough votes to win a seat—despite the SYL's efforts— many people believed the voting had been rigged. They vented their frustrations on the district commissioner and the district judge, who had ratified the results and certified the election as free and fair.

The Coup of 1969

The 1969 election polarized Somalia and created tremendous animosity toward the civilian government. There was a widespread perception of a tainted election, and the clan feuds sullied the reputation of the government of President Abdirashid Ali Sharmarke and Prime Minister Mohamed Hagi Ibrahim Egal. On October 15, President Sharmarke was assassinated by his bodyguard, a police officer in Las Anod much to the shock of the nation.

Less than a week later, on October 21, while the nation was still mourning the death of the president, the Somali military, under the leadership of Major General Mohamed Siad Barre, were able to take over without a single shot being fired. Siad Barre was a masterful tactician who raised no suspicion of a coup until the timing was perfect. In using mostly junior officers to carry out his military plot, he avoided involving those who were close to him in rank. He was well aware that they could either foil the plot or frustrate his ambition of reaching the proverbial mountain.

Most observers did not expect Siad Barre to be the dominant figure in this group. He was a relatively old officer, with more than two dozen children, and had never displayed any disposition to usurp the power of the government. He was considered subservient and quite docile, with an unassuming personality, and was thought to have neither the character nor the temperament to engineer and undertake such a daunting coup. But the doubters were proved wrong as it became evident that the old man had long harbored an ambition to take over and had simply been waiting for the right moment to strike.

I was in the third grade when the military took over in Somalia, and I vividly remember that fateful day. Early that morning we arrived at school and, as we did every morning, were getting ready for the morning parade to sing the national anthem. Suddenly our school principal announced that a military revolution had occurred and that all classes were cancelled until further notice. He dismissed the students and told us to go home and stay indoors. We did not fully understand what he meant, but somehow got the point that something out of the ordinary had taken place. As we scattered toward our homes, men in military uniforms spread out over the city. Every alley and backstreet was filled with men carrying rifles, but otherwise the streets were deserted. For two or three days, there was a complete lockdown of the city and all commercial and social activities came to a standstill. However, after those few days, we simply went back to our normal routine. Our mundane life continued unabated, and we resumed our classes in the Dusamareb elementary school. The change in the political leadership had no discernible effect on our daily lives.

As a third-grader, I didn't know what to make of this event. Most of the elders I overheard discussing it were amused about the change in government. They often called it tawra, the Arabic word for revolution, and wondered who might be its leader. Radio Mogadishu played nationalist songs nonstop but made no announcement about either the identity of the new leader or the composition of the group that had taken over. Later, the news was released that Siad Barre, the leader of the Supreme Revolutionary Council (SRC), including the army and mostly junior police officers, had seized power.

On hearing this, Somalis welcomed the coup and hailed the takeover as timely and necessary. There was a euphoric expectation that the new military government would restore civility and order and continue the country's path toward democracy. The euphoria was, however, short-lived. Immediately after coming to power, Siad Barre dissolved Parliament and suspended the constitution. The new military rulers imposed draconian measures curbing many of the freedoms previously enjoyed by Somalis. Among these measures was the criminalization of any public reference to clan: a mention of clan could now land a Somali in prison. The SRC also issued decrees imposing the death penalty for murder. Siad Barre made the point by executing a close member of his sub-clan for a capital offense that had been committed before the coup.

Not surprisingly, people became fearful of the military. Clan disputes dissipated, and most citizens became apprehensive about the policies of the new regime. Nevertheless Dusamareb became safe and secure, and a peaceful environment prevailed throughout the country for the first few years of the new regime. As a child, although I was not able to analyze the situation, I felt the difference. The military takeover seemed to be a good thing. It meant no more fighting and no more clan quarrels. The imposition of the death penalty appeared to lessen revenge killings over clan disputes in the countryside. There seemed to be no more senseless killing, and our safety and security appeared to improve.

The elders in my family did not share my innocent optimism, and soon our livelihood was affected by the new regime's policies and politics. In October 1970, Somalia adopted "scientific socialism" and embarked on a new trajectory, essentially joining the Cold War. The new policies negatively affected free enterprise and the market economy that had been put in place and encouraged by the previous regime. In October 1971, two years after Siad Barre's coup, the government nationalized all privately owned businesses, including banks, insurance companies, and factories.

The change of policies was immediately felt in the commercial activities that supported our household. My uncle knew two lines of business very well—importing cigarettes and importing sugar—and both of these activities were nationalized. The government created a national agency for the importation of sugar and a monopoly for the importation and distribution of cigarettes, so my uncle's commercial activity squeaked to a halt. He was limited to selling only a few retail items here and there. Eventually he became a low-level employee of a national agency created by the government.

The fall from thriving businessman to minor civil servant made my uncle personally bitter. It affected his political outlook negatively as well. Like many others, he developed anti-revolutionary feelings. He did not voice loud objections, but practiced soft opposition. Fortunately, although he was emotionally and morally devastated, this had no discernible impact on his relationships with his immediate family.

Nevertheless our family lifestyle and our standard of living deteriorated quickly. To me it seemed paradoxical and quite absurd: we had safety, we had security. There was no more clan-versus-clan—no more fighting in the city between the Ayr and Marehan sub-clans, rivalries that had adversely affected our livelihood. But I did not grasp the magnitude of the devastation felt by my uncle. I didn't know enough to ask where the bread came from. Whether my uncle brought it home as a government employee or as a businessman didn't matter to me.

The 1970s: A Time of Reckoning

Growing up in Dusamareb in the 1970s, I was optimistic and hopeful about the future. I had an insatiable appetite to learn, but I never aspired to such elite professions as doctor or engineer. The only profession I cherished was teaching. My teachers in my formative years had an immeasurable influence on me, and later on, in high school, I also developed a feeling for politics. I became politically conscious and inadvertently became an armchair politician. I developed a knack for political debate, acquired leftist leanings, and enjoyed reading Marxist literature such as Das Kapital and The Political Economy of Socialism. I became fond of dialectical materialism and was on the edge of becoming an atheist. Reading these and similar books sharpened my analytical skills, and I became a critic of the military regime. Gradually, I came around to my uncle's point of view.

My growing political awareness coincided with deterioration of the political situation in Somalia. In 1977–78, the country fought a devastating war with Ethiopia and lost miserably. It was counterintuitive for Somalia to invade Ethiopia at that time: Ethiopia also had a socialist political system, and the two nations shared a common ideology. But we were socialists in name rather than in practice. Most Somalis steadfastly supported the "liberation" of the Somali-inhabited area of Ethiopia from this perceived enemy. We were all under the illusion that it was incumbent on every Somali to participate in the noble cause of saving our kith and kin from the yoke of Ethiopian colonialism for the sake of a greater Somalia.

The defeat took its toll on the morale of the Somali military. Following an abortive military coup on April 9, 1978, led by officers who were infuriated by the defeat and the way the war effort had been handled, seventeen officers were executed. Although no one clan was responsible for the putsch, Siad Barre accused members of the Majertein clan of being the perpetrators. They were branded as subversives and counter-revolutionaries.

Most of Somalia's high-ranking Majertein officers were sacked, and a good number of senior civil servants were relieved of their duties. The word Majertein became synonymous with "traitor"— an absurd idea, but Siad Barre and his clique resorted to this tactic to dispel public disappointment about their conduct of government affairs. The regime committed heinous acts of violence first against the Majertein in central and northeast Somalia and later against the Isaaq clan in the northwest. Thus, it seemed that the only option for getting rid of this regime was a resort to clan politics.

The economy began to falter due to the regime's dismal fiscal, monetary, and trade policies. Somalia, with its limited domestic revenue, required a small but efficient government, but by the late 1970s it had a bloated bureaucracy. Government had become the biggest employer and the biggest provider of services. It had fallen into the trap of believing that the size of its military and bureaucracy was a reflection of its power.

In its approach to trade, Siad Barre's government pursued a closed commercial policy. This led to a severe shortage of commodities in the market and high prices for most goods, taking them out of the reach of the mainstream families. Government subsidies were reduced due to the shortage of money, and food aid also declined. Inflation persistently increased, and the value of the Somali shilling plummeted.

Leaving Home

In 1979, after graduating from high school, I completed three months of military training at the Halane military training facility. This "boot camp" was followed by a year of national service as a teacher in Adado, a small town in central Somalia, ninety kilometers north of Dusamareb. There were very few teachers in Adado at that time, so the people of the town received me very well. The headmaster of the school was often absent and had a hands-off policy in dealing with the teaching staff. I had a heavy load of teaching, essentially teaching almost everything, and though I had no formal training I became very good at it. Teaching gave me a sense of what to expect in my future endeavors. It was a tough job, dealing daily with children, but it was also very rewarding. After five months in Adado, I was transferred to Dusamareb, where I spent the remaining period of my national service.

After the year of national service, I applied to the Somali National University to study economics. Although I was good at "hard science" and had the required grades, I found the social sciences more interesting. The university's admission test was fair and the entrance exam was thankfully free of the corrupt practices that permeated many other areas of the public service. Space was limited, and only those who proved their knowledge through tests were admitted. I passed the test and was admitted to the Faculty of Economics, among thirty other students admitted to the faculty that year. They were mostly fresh from high school, but a few had enrolled after serving in the public service or the military. We became a close-knit group, and many of us are still connected.

The language of instruction at the university was Italian; most of the professors were either Italians or Somalis with an Italian background, and they spoke no language but Italian. Like the majority of the students, I spoke hardly any Italian, so I enrolled in a six-month Italian immersion course. On the first day of class, the professor approached me and asked, "Come ti chiami?"—"What is your name?" Knowing no Italian, I was not able to respond and simply stared at her. That is how I began my study of the Italian language. This method of teaching forced me to work hard—it was the best way to learn a foreign language.

Six months later I was able to study economics using this fresh and novel language. The Mogadishu environment also helped—Italian was commonly spoken in the city because southern Somalia had been an Italian colony from the late 1800s until 1960. Italian had once been the lingua franca and was the administrative language of Somalia before the Somali script was introduced in 1972. Learning Italian had the added benefit that I was now able to understand Italian movies and read Italian literature. It also added to the other languages that I was able to read and write—Arabic and English.

I studied the theory of market economy and took courses in scientific socialism, such as the political economy of socialism. The university also had a few professors from American universities, so not surprisingly many of the economics courses compared Somalia's socialism with various aspects of market economies—resource management, the theory of the firm, public finance, macroeconomics and microeconomics, and so on. These courses offered a completely different view of what was being practiced by Somalia's socialist government. Although I had been a firm believer in the international labor movement, I began to see that socialism in Somalia had outlived its usefulness and that Somali culture was antithetical to the political canons of scientific socialism. Somalis are commercially skillful, inherently capitalist, and highly industrious—a great advantage to the Somali diaspora all over the world.

Nevertheless, whatever socialism's merits, education in Somalia, from elementary school to university, was free; I never paid a dime for the quality education I received. I am grateful for this opportunity that socialist Somalia gave its son. Coming from a poor nomadic family, I could not have afforded my university education without government support. Not only were tuition and room and board taken care of, but students were also provided with pocket money and the services of a free health clinic on campus. Had I not been admitted to a government-owned and government-run university, I would have had no means to go abroad in later years.

In 1979, Somalia's high schools graduated around nine hundred students, less than half of whom were admitted to the Somali National University. There was an economic boom under way in Arabia, and those lucky enough to get a passport and visa went abroad and made a considerable amount of money there. Some others who were not admitted to university or who were unwilling to pursue higher education started their own businesses, but many were given jobs in the public sector. The government was at that time the biggest employer in Somalia, and high school graduates received jobs without having to undertake a complex application process. Of course, this explained why the government bureaucracy became bloated.

I graduated from the Somali National University in late 1984 and applied for a job at the Ministry of Finance. Although I had graduated with honors, it was not easy to get a job with the ministry. Its employees were paid very high salaries, so successful applicants needed recommendations from politically connected people. There were many hurdles to overcome: I had to enlist the help of an aunt, who knew another aunt, who in turn knew the director general of the ministry. In early 1985, I succeeded and was hired.

Like many Somali ministries, the Ministry of Finance was overstaffed at the time; there were only a limited numbers of jobs to be done. Most of its employees merely drew their salaries and passed time at the ministry headquarters. I joined the ranks of the underutilized staff, following a routine of showing up for work at around 9 a.m., chatting with colleagues, and then heading home for lunch around 1 p.m. The afternoons were similar—I was merely drawing a salary, and that was the state of affairs in most of the departments of the Somali government at that time.

Abdullahi Warsame Nur, a lawyer and veteran colonel who served as the auditor general and assistant minister of finance, did not get along with the minister of finance, as they did not see eye-to-eye in the conduct of ministry affairs. The powerful minister had relieved his assistant minister of all his responsibilities. Thus Abdullahi had plenty of time on his hands. As a low-level employee of the Ministry of Finance, I used to complain to Abdullahi about the lack of work, not knowing that he was in the same predicament. But I also provided him with documentation on reforms that we might undertake to be both more productive and more efficient. Sensing that I was trying to be proactive, Abdullahi appreciated the assistance—so much so that when the revenue section of the Ministry of Finance became the new Ministry of Revenue in August 1985 and he became the minister of revenue, he appointed me director of the excise tax department.

Excise tax, sometimes called "sin tax," is a tax on items such as sugar, cigarettes, alcohol, and gasoline. It has a dual purpose: on the one hand to reduce the consumption of these goods, and on the other hand to generate state revenue from the sale of these goods. In the developed world, it is an "earmarked" tax, in which, for example, the tax on gasoline helps finance the construction and maintenance of roads, while taxes on sugar, cigarettes, and alcohol support healthcare expenditures.

Most of my colleagues and coworkers could not believe my rapid promotion—from being a recent university graduate with a minimum of experience to my appointment as director of a department. The rumor mill went into full gear, with some saying that I was related to the minister, whereas in fact Abdullahi was a member of the Abgal sub-clan of the Hawiye clan while I am from the Majertein sub-clan of the Darod clan. Abdullahi was a patriotic Somali, free from clannism and never showing a preference for a particular group. Out of his thoughtfulness, humanity, and Somali-ness, he gave me an opportunity to be a director.

I returned the favor by working hard and being faithful to him. Now I came to work at 7 a.m. and left at 3 p.m., sometimes returning later in the afternoon to do an extra few hours of work and respond to correspondence. Abdullahi and I became very close and developed a collegial relationship.

Earlier, however, in a hiatus period when I was not doing much at the Ministry of Finance, I had started looDking for graduate scholarships. I had been eager to pursue graduate studies because my career at the ministry was not looking promising. One of the few available scholarships from the West was the African Graduate Fellowship Program (AFGRAD), sponsored by the African-American Institute (AAI) and partially funded by the United States Agency for International Development (USAID). The only application requirement was that applicants be recent university graduates and government employees—two conditions I easily satisfied. This was a competitive scholarship, and making it onto the list of candidates was quite a challenge. There would be exams, but to become eligible, applicants needed the Ministry of Higher Education to add their names to the list of candidates.

By the time I became aware of these scholarships, I was a director at the Ministry of Revenue. I had the use of a government vehicle, employed a driver, and was living the Somali dream. Nevertheless, the prospect of advancing my education in the West was an attractive one. I went to the Ministry of Higher Education and submitted my application for a scholarship and a supporting letter from my employer.

There were sixty-six names on the list of applicants, competing for five positions. The Ministry of Higher Education procedure for shortlisting the candidates included an oral interview conducted by five officials: Abdi Farah, director general of the ministry; Abdullahi Anshur, also from the ministry; Gail Baker, from the AAI; Ed Toll, USAID representative in Somalia; and Abdi Hussein Girreh, also of USAID.

The committee asked where in the United States I wanted to pursue my graduate studies. I replied confidently, "UCLA." They asked me why, and I replied, "I've been told that California is like Somalia and has warm weather." In reality, I was afraid of what snow and cold might be like. I thought that ice, as I knew it from the refrigerator, might be falling out of the sky elsewhere in the United

States. The committee, when they realized that this was the only reason I had picked UCLA, broke out in laughter. I sensed that my chances of being accepted had improved, although I was not sure why.

Then the committee looked at transcripts, and of the sixty-six applicants, they selected ten—five primary and five secondary candidates. If something happened to the primary candidates, or if any of them withdrew their candidacy, the secondary candidates would fill their place. I was ranked number nine. It was a long shot; I was thinking that, for me to have a chance, something terrible had to happen to four of the primary candidates. But the committee took all ten profiles to the USAID and AAI's executive committee, which included the deans of all the schools offering scholarships to AFGRAD. That committee would choose the successful candidates, considering criteria such as transcripts and the results of standardized tests such as the Test of English as a Foreign Language (TOEFL) and the Graduate Record Examination (GRE). Fortunately I had one of the highest grades in both the TOEFL and the GRE. I had made it into the final five!

One of the members of the executive committee was Dean Hamilton, of the College of Arts and Science at Vanderbilt University in Nashville, Tennessee. A down-to-earth African American, Dean Hamilton selected me as the most suitable candidate for Vanderbilt. I would receive a full scholarship plus a small stipend to cover the cost of my rent, food, and other incidentals. In addition, I would remain on the Somali government payroll and my family would receive my full salary.

Dr. Abdiweli Mohamed Ali Prime meets with Secretary-General Ban Ki-moon (right) Minister of the Transitional Federal Government of the Somali Republic September 24, 2011 United Nations, New York UN Photo/Paulo Filgueiras

Prime Minister Abdiweli Mohamed Ali Press Conference February 21, 2012, the European Commission HQ, Brussels

Both Somalia and I would make history in Vanderbilt University: Somalia would become the eighty-seventh country to have one of its citizens attend Vanderbilt, and I would be the first Somali to study there.

ONE FOOT IN AMERICA:

GRADUATE STUDIES IN THE UNITED STATES, TURMOIL IN SOMALIA

Getting Acquainted with the New World

I was slated to join Vanderbilt University's graduate program in economic development in the fall of 1986. When I left Somalia for the United States in August of that year, it was the first time I had ever flown in an airplane. I was accompanied by Abdullahi Godah Barre, who had won an AFGRAD fellowship to attend the University of Illinois at Carbondale. Abdullahi was few years older than I and had flown before, so he was amused by my lack of traveling experience. He found it very entertaining that I couldn't even figure out how to turn off the overhead cold air flow in the airplane, and I don't remember him offering me any assistance! Nevertheless we spent a pleasant orientation week together in New York City.

Abdullahi and I were booked to stay at the Tudor Hotel, a five-star establishment whose rooms were elegant and spacious. We spent most of the time in the hotel, watching too much TV and leaving only to grab lunch or spend a few hours at the African American Institute office in Manhattan. Abdullahi continued to enjoy my lack of experience with technology. I had never watched television in Somalia, so I was not familiar with the concept of TV commercials. One day, as we were watching a TV drama, a Coca-Cola commercial came on screen. I had been following the story closely, and the sudden appearance of the soft-drink commercial baffled me. Exasperated, I said to Abdullahi, "What's going on? This doesn't make sense!" I could not understand how the commercial fit into the story. Abdullahi, of course, found my confusion hilarious.

Eventually we decided it was time to leave the hotel and explore the city. We decided to go out for breakfast. We were bewildered by the speed of the traffic and took at least fifteen minutes to cross the street. But we were happy to find an Italian restaurant because we both knew a bit of Italian; at least we could order Italian food for breakfast. Little did we know that Italian restaurants in the United States do not necessarily carry out business in Italian. When I saw the menu—prime rib steak, eggs, French fries—there was nothing I could recognize except eggs. So I ordered scrambled eggs, toast, and orange juice.

Abdullahi, still acting the experienced traveler, said: "You're in New York City and you're ordering eggs for breakfast? You can do better than that." I replied, "But I only know eggs, so I have ordered eggs." I wouldn't budge. Abdullahi ordered New York steak, and when it arrived it was rare—not the type of the steak we knew in Somalia. When Abdullahi sliced the steak, blood oozed out. Now I was the one who was laughing; I had fun telling him that he could have ordered scrambled eggs just like I had.

After breakfast, on our way back to the hotel, we saw a man taking money from a wall. At least, that is what we thought we saw. He faced the wall and put his card in a slot, then typed in a code of sorts, and money came out of another slot. Neither Abdullahi nor I had any concept of an ATM, so we leaned over the man's shoulder to watch this strange thing he was doing.

This would have been completely normal behavior back in Somalia. But imagine two black strangers looking over the shoulder of a white American who is receiving money from an ATM. Angry and afraid, he turned to us and said, "What are you staring at?" I said, "We're just looking." He was clearly furious, but we didn't understand why he was so annoyed. I repeated, "It's okay! We're just looking." But finally we understood that our behavior was bothering him, and we left. It was incredible to us; no one was dispensing money from behind the machine, and the bank was not even open, yet the man had just walked up to the wall and taken money out of it!

After a week of orientation and similarly novel experiences, it was time for Abdullahi and I to leave New York. I went to Nashville, while Abdullahi headed for Carbondale. By then, I had learned at least a few things about America: what a TV commercial was and how to operate an ATM.

Arriving in Nashville

When I arrived in Nashville, I felt wealthy: I had $3,600, of which $1,800 was a month's traveling allowance from the Ministry of Finance of Somalia and an additional $1,800 from the African American Institute to defray my initial settlement cost. Those were the "good old days" in Somalia, when traveling government employees were given a per diem of $80 a day. In Nashville, the Vanderbilt staff helped me to open a checking account at the Third National Bank, and I finally received an ATM card of my own.

Vanderbilt is a university with a good academic reputation and sometimes brags about being "the Harvard of the South." I considered myself lucky to be attending such a school. I was enrolled in the Graduate Program of Economic Development (GPED), which had begun in 1956 and included students from all over the world. When I arrived in the fall of 1986, the GPED had a large contingent of students from Turkey and South Korea.

My first few weeks in Nashville were not easy. University students in America either spend a lot of money eating out, or they learn to cook; cooking one's own meals can makes a huge difference to the pocketbook. Unfortunately, cooking skills came very slowly to me. It also turned out that my bank was located between a Kentucky Fried Chicken (KFC) outlet and a restaurant serving delicious catfish. So I developed a routine: I would go to the bank, withdraw some money, and dine at either KFC or the catfish restaurant. If I had lunch at KFC, I would have dinner at the catfish place. I was spending too much money on food, and my financial reserve at the Third National Bank was dwindling.

I was, however, fortunate once again. Although I was the only Somali student at Vanderbilt at the time, there was a Somali family living in Nashville: the three sons and one daughter of Abdiaziz Nur Hersi, a staunch Somali nationalist. A former member of the Somali Parliament in the 1960s, Abdiaziz Nur Hersi later became a cabinet member in the military regime of Siad Barre. His children, Dr. Abdirahman Abdiaziz, Dahir Abdiaziz, Omar Abdiaziz, and Munira Abdiaziz, received me in Nashville with much kindheartedness. It was Munira who rescued me from my financial predicament and taught me how to cook a few dishes and prepare her delicious signature sauce.

The Nur Hersi family, who had arrived in the United States in the early 1980s, unlocked the secrets of America for me by bringing me to places I would not have visited on my own. While Munira was teaching me how to cook, Dahir was taking me to clubs on Friday nights, plunging me into their culture. Abdirahman, meanwhile, was the wise guy of the family, always warning me about the dark side of American life and the dangers to watch out for; he was a father figure for all of us.

When I had told people in Somalia that I would be studying in Nashville, many of them were surprised and wary. "Why are you going to Nashville?" they would ask. "It's the center of the Ku Klux Klan." The KKK, as it is also known, is a radical group of white supremacists predominantly found in the southern part of the United States who believe that the "Aryan race" is the superior race and that everyone else is inferior. But Nashville was a welcoming city. The city is home to a large number of black people and has more than a touch of "southern hospitality." I didn't feel any sort of prejudice or discrimination, either subtle or blatant. The residents were very cordial and very receptive to visitors. I had the best time in America while living in Nashville.

Although the city is diverse and multi-cultured, the student body at Vanderbilt was 96 percent white. I didn't feel different and "black," but I did feel like a foreigner when others noticed my accent. They often asked where I was from. My response generated an interesting conversation, both about Somalia in particular and Africa in general. I became different, exotic—not just "black," but a stranger from a faraway land. To Americans my name was quite distinctive, and it was very difficult for some of them to pronounce it correctly. I have never understood why Abdiweli is more difficult to pronounce than Schwarzenegger, but apparently it is. So I asked those who found it difficult to call me Mr. Ali. At least they were familiar with the name because of their familiarity with the boxer Muhammad Ali.

I did have difficulty with the southern American accent that is common in Nashville. A few of my professors had a southern drawl, and even people from the northern states have a hard time understanding people from Texas or Alabama, let alone people from Africa. Academically, however, I had no problem. The staff at the GPED made my transition easy; they were considerate and accommodating throughout the transition process, picking me up from the airport and settling me in a dorm, and helping me buy necessities such as bed sheets, pillows, and other household items. They gave me a good sense of Vanderbilt and of Nashville. GPED director James Worley and his assistant, Marilyn Whiteman, were particularly supportive. Marilyn and James also assigned a senior graduate student to help me out after work hours.

I lived in the graduate dorms at Lewis House. Living in close proximity to the classes and the library helped me to integrate fully into the American university environment. Within a few weeks, I was a Tennessean ... minus, of course, the accent.

Academic Life at Vanderbilt

The GPED had, on average, an enrolment of thirty to forty students every year. The program was part of the economics department, one of the largest departments at the college of arts and science. It introduced me to the education, culture, and lifestyle of the United States. Through it, I became thoroughly acquainted with capitalism and the market economy, continuing the introduction that had begun at Somali National University.

I enrolled in a microeconomics course taught by an Indian professor, Gian Singh Sahota, who was a tough grader and held his students to high standards. My other great professors at Vanderbilt included Andrea Maneschi, an Australian of Italian origin, who taught international economics; Samuel Morley, who had spent a good deal of time in Latin America and taught macroeconomics and the policies and programs of economic development; and Katherine Anderson, a tough but amiable teacher of statistics. Almost every student failed her first statistics test. Bill Thweatt taught us the history of economics. Clive Bell, a conservative British professor who had previously served at the World Bank, taught public finance. One of the finest professors I had was Kaushik Basu, a visiting professor from the Delhi School of Economics. Relatively young and a rising star in the field of economics, he was a prolific writer and had published seminal articles at an early age. Now that I was living in the West, I could relate to the theories my professors taught. Their courses reflected the market environment in which we lived.

As the former director of the excise tax department in Somalia's Ministry of Revenue, I was eager to make my academic work at Vanderbilt University applicable to Somalia. My dissertation, "The Possibility of a Tax Reform Program in Somalia," dealt with the fact that Somalia's taxation system needed serious reform. The system was outdated and not responsive to the country's changing economic environment. Some of Somalia's tax laws dated from Italian colonial times, and as a result Somalia in the 1980s was using a tax system that had originated in the 1920s.

I wanted a Somali tax system that related to the current economic situation of Somalia—a tax system that was fair, efficient, and equitable, and that took into account the macroeconomic framework and distribution of income in the country. I also wanted a system that was adaptable and flexible. For example, most of the tax that I was in charge of, excise tax, was specific: it was a tax on the unit, not on the value. For example, in the purchase of a package of cigarettes, the tax was collected on the pack but not on the value of the cigarettes. In a high-inflationary environment such as Somalia's, the price of cigarettes was continuously increasing, but the government was collecting the same amount of tax year in, year out. As a result, it was generating the same amount of revenue from the item even though the value of the commodity had tripled or quadrupled. To generate more revenue, the tax code had to take price fluctuations into account. It could, for example, have administered an ad valorem tax, which is based on a percentage of the value of an item.

There was a need for reform not only in excise taxes, but also in the tax system as a whole, including personal income taxes, corporate taxes, sales taxes, profit taxes, and all the minor taxes collected at the time. I was optimistic that the knowledge I gained from my studies in finance and economics at Vanderbilt could be put to good use in reforming the Somali tax system.

America in the Late 1980s

Although Nashville and Vanderbilt University exposed me to a different system of governance, but that system was not completely new to me. It was in some ways similar to the one I had known as a child—albeit for a brief moment in 1960s Somalia—which had given me my first idea of how democracy works. The majority of my youth, however, was spent under a dictatorship, and I had no real understanding of liberal democracy. At Vanderbilt, I learned the difference between autocratic regimes such as Somalia's and open societies like that of the United States. In only a few years, my political outlook was completely transformed.

I arrived in the United States at the height of the controversial Iran Contra Affair. The United States had been selling arms to Iran to help free U.S. hostages being held by Hezbollah rebels in Lebanon. The income from the sale was intended to fund a Nicaraguan guerrilla group, the Contras, to fight against the socialist government of Nicaragua. At the same time, a U.S. congressional law clearly stated that it was illegal for the United States to give or sell arms to the Contras.

During this scandal, Barbara Walters, a popular talk-show host, interviewed U.S. President Ronald Reagan to discuss the Iran Contra Affair. Ms. Walters was very tenacious in the interview, asking penetrating and powerful questions. President Reagan tried to avoid answering her questions, as this would have added fuel to the fire. He had a tendency to frustrate reporters by pretending that he had difficulty in hearing the question. He would hold his fingers behind his earlobes and say, "Please repeat the question," unyielding to the barrage of questions from the reporters.

In this interview, Ms. Walters finally became exasperated. Pointing her finger at President Reagan, she said, "Mr. President, will you answer my question?"

That was a watershed moment in my understanding of the difference between a dictatorship and a liberal democracy. That a simple journalist could address the president of the most powerful country in the world, and in such a direct manner, astonished me. I was trying to imagine a journalist interviewing Siad Barre, the autocratic ruler of Somalia, and challenging him in the way that Barbara Walters was addressing President Reagan. This would have been tantamount to treason, and that journalist would never have been seen or heard from again.

Oddly enough, initially I was annoyed with Ms. Walters. Consider my background and the circumstances in which I was raised: in Somalia at the time, Siad Barre controlled everything. He had developed a personality cult and cultivated an aura of invisibility. He had all kinds of names—the victor, the father, the visionary leader, the erudite far-sighted vanguard, and so on—so much so that many Somalis of my generation had internalized Siad Barre's image of himself. Thus, for a journalist to ask him pointed questions would have been unacceptable behavior to most Somalis.

Within few months, though, I had come to terms with the power of the press in a liberal democracy. I was no longer angry with Barbara Walters or with the idea of someone holding the president accountable. I became well versed in the democratic traditions and the political party system of the United States. I closely followed the election of November 1988, when the Republican candidate George H.W. Bush ran against the Democratic Party candidate, Michael Dukakis. Bush easily won the election, but the fact that a second-generation Greek-American could contest the highest office in the land, regardless of who ultimately won, was to me as significant as the election itself.

Jesse Jackson, an African-American activist, became prominent in the Democratic primaries before that election, and he had been winning key states such as Michigan and South Carolina. For a time he led the Democratic forces, including such high-profile politicians as Al Gore and Michael Dukakis, and was sweeping some vital areas in the south. It was captivating and quite mesmerizing for me to watch the journey of this young African American long before Obama came on the U.S. political scene. Jesse Jackson was the embodiment of a quintessential black politician in America, a trailblazer who cleared the road for Obama to ascend to the highest seat in the land. Observing that election and Jackson's spectacular performance, I knew that it was only a matter of time before a man of color would occupy the White House.

I became fascinated with the electoral system of the United States. Somalis had had no exposure to democracy and elections since the military takeover of 1969. The only elections they had experienced were those in which there was only one candidate's name on the ballot, and that name was Siad Barre. The results of the election were known before the votes were cast, and 99 percent of the voters were regularly claimed to have voted for the all-knowing, all-powerful president. It was said that, whenever Saddam Hussein would "run" for re-election in Iraq, he would be told that 99 percent of Iraqis had voted for him—and that he then would say: "Bring me the 1 percent." This summed up the essence of dictatorship in Somalia as well.

Somalia under Tyranny

While I was in the United States in the late 1980s, dramatic events were occurring back home in Somalia. The Somali Nationalist Movement (SNM), an armed opposition group dominated by leaders of the Isaaq clan of northern Somalia, attacked key population centers such as Hargeisa, the largest city in the north, and Burao, another large northern city. There was a swift, severe, and disproportionate reaction from the Somali government. The fallout from this reaction was quite devastating, resulting in the deaths of untold numbers of innocent civilians.

Images of women and children fleeing from the bombardment of Hargeisa and Burao, of refugees running to escape to Ethiopia, were broadcast everywhere. Even though Somalis in the United States were watching these events from afar, the situation was unnerving. The SNM had been reckless and irresponsible in taking its operations to heavily populated centers, but even so, to see the government killing its own people in assaults from the air was extremely upsetting.

Nevertheless, most of my colleagues supported the government because they were apprehensive about the possibility of Somalia breaking up. They assumed that the SNM had secessionist ambitions and argued that it was the duty of the government of Somalia to defend the nation's territorial integrity. In their opinion, the government had done the right thing and had no choice but to act as it did.

My reaction was different. I felt that the government was neither representative nor legitimate. It was a military regime that held power by the barrel of the gun and was unyielding both to the opposition and to popular demands. It used brutal force unnecessarily to suppress dissent. Many civilians were branded as subversives and traitors, and dissenters had been arrested from the very beginning of the regime.

Even in the early 1980s, the government had used brutal force in Mudug, in central Somalia, following an abortive coup. The coup had been spearheaded by officers disgruntled with Somalia's defeat by Ethiopia in the Ogaden war of 1977–78. In response, the Somali army had attacked Siad Barre's perceived enemies, the Majertein clan, who had been prominent in the civilian administration preceding the military regime—two prime ministers and a president of the civilian administration were members of this clan. Although military officers of all backgrounds and across the clan spectrum had taken part in the coup, Siad Barre aimed at decommissioning and arresting the majority of the Majertein officers. He also targeted the civilian population of this clan in Mudug.

The repressive tone of the revolutionary government would be set here. The Red Berets systematically smashed the small reservoirs in the area around Galkayo so as to deny them water and their herds. In the space of a month, over 2,000 people in the Galkayo area perished by thirst.

By masking the reasons for Somalia's defeat and misconstruing the coup as the work of a particular clan that had ulterior political motives, the Siad Bare regime tried to absolve itself of responsibility for addressing the nation's underlying political problems. As a result, in February 1979 the first armed Somali opposition group, the Somali Salvation Democratic Front (SSDF), was formed and based in Ethiopia. Abdullahi Yusuf, the leader of the SSDF, had been one of the lead commanders in the war with Ethiopia. In March 1981, the Somali National Movement (SNM) followed suit and likewise was based in Ethiopia. It was an irony that Ethiopia, which a few years earlier had fought a devastating war with Somalia, later hosted the same officers who had once fired at it from the other side of the trenches.

The United States, which had been the main supporter of Siad Barre since he had broken his ties with the Soviet Union in 1977, had underwritten Siad's military after Ethiopia turned to the Soviet Union for support. Eventually, however, when it recognized that Siad's regime was brutally suppressing its own people, it cut off all military and non-military support to Somalia. By the end of the 1980s, Somalia was disintegrating, its government was crumbling and losing legitimacy, and its military officers were deserting in droves. No one, however, expected that the government would fall within two years.

My Return to Somalia

While Somalia was falling apart, I was completing my studies at Vanderbilt University. After graduating in the summer of 1988, I wondered whether it would be better for me to stay in the United States or go back to Somalia. Finally I decided to return, for two reasons.

First, I had entered the United States on an exchange student (J1) visa, with an explicit stipulation that I return to Somalia after graduation and spend a minimum of two years there before reentering the United States. I could only have remained in the United States illegally, and that was not an option for me.

Second, the only viable alternative for me to stay legally in the United States was to apply for political asylum. This seemed to be a remote possibility: I had been a mid-level government employee in Somalia, the director of a department, and had come to the United States on a Somali government scholarship. Thus, I had no convincing case to apply for political asylum.

Nonetheless, I did have a third option up my sleeve, just in case the other options evaporated. While still enrolled in the master's program at Vanderbilt, I had applied to enter Ph.D. programs in perhaps a dozen U.S. universities. My applications had a dual purpose: not only to pursue further graduate studies, but also to return to the United States legally.

Most of my friends, including those facing similar predicaments, thought I was not in my right mind to consider going back to Somalia. The situation in the country was rapidly deteriorating—politically, socially, and economically—and it was about to explode. My family was of the same opinion and repeatedly advised me not to return. They expressed concerns that the Somalia I would be returning to was completely different from the one I left two years earlier. I refused to listen and, against all odds, decided to go back.

I arrived in Mogadishu on October 18, 1988, and immediately saw the truth in my family's admonition that Somalia had changed drastically. My biggest shock was witnessing the extent to which the standard of living had fallen in just two years. When I left Somalia, the exchange rate had been around 70 Somali shillings per U.S. dollar; upon my return, the exchange rate hovered around 200 shillings per dollar. A plate of pasta that in a restaurant would have cost a dozen shillings in 1986 had quadrupled in price; that change was a microcosm of the state of the economy and reflected the beginning of a much more serious economic situation. By early 1990, the Somali shilling was to depreciate to a rate of 4,500 per U.S. dollar, rendering it almost worthless.

Within only a few weeks, I realized that the situation was untenable and decided to return to America. I was anxiously awaiting responses from the universities I had applied to for pursuing Ph.D. studies. Fortunately, I was offered an appealing admission package from the University of Connecticut at Storrs, including a tuition waiver and a modest stipend to cover my living expenses.

Wanting to return to the United States as soon as possible, I applied to enroll in a two-month public finance course at the International Monetary Fund (IMF) Institute in Washington, D.C. As an employee of the Somali Ministry of Revenue, I was readily accepted and granted a G2 visa. This was my ticket back to America, and I intended to remain there until the situation improved in Somalia. The IMF program ran from June to August 1989, just in time for me to begin my Ph.D. studies at the University of Connecticut in the fall.

After arriving in June 1989, I stayed in Washington for two months to connect with old friends and acquaintances. I then moved to Storrs to commence my graduate studies. Meanwhile, the situation in Somalia was deteriorating even more. Fighting broke out in Mogadishu between protesters and government troops in July. Scores of people, including a senior military officer, were shot and killed. Once again, the government launched a massive crackdown against those it perceived to be the perpetrators. On July 17, government troops in Jazeera, on the outskirts of Mogadishu, executed forty-seven innocent civilians, most of them belonging to the Isaaq clan.

Because of the worsening situation in Somalia, I was disheartened and had difficulty sleeping. Though I was in the United States, It was difficult for me to concentrate, this at a time when I had to be at my best both mentally and physically. I could not disengage myself from the tragedy occurring at home.

Seeking Political Asylum

I decided to postpone my studies, and look for a job. I left Storrs and returned to Washington. Since I was determined eventually to resume my studies, I decided to apply for political asylum, the only avenue toward legal residency. Ironically, my chances of obtaining asylum improved as the situation in Somalia deteriorated to the point where the government lost complete control of the country except for Mogadishu and a few other major towns.

Back in Washington, I looked for a job without having a work permit. Fortunately my social security card indicated that I was permitted to work. Another reason for my return to Washington was to visit Hodan Said Isse, whom I was courting at the time. Hodan had arrived in Washington a year earlier and had been granted political asylum in the United States. Since we were in a similar situation, she encouraged me to submit my application for asylum. She had also come to the United States on a government scholarship and by way of an exchange student (J1) visa. I surmised that if she had been granted asylum, my prospects should even be better because of the current situation in Somalia.

Hodan introduced me to Allan Ebert, the Somali community's favorite lawyer in the District of Columbia area. He had helped quite a number of Somalis in their asylum cases. I paid the required fee, filled out the necessary forms, and submitted my application. Within a few weeks, I was granted an interview with the U.S. Immigration and Naturalization Service (INS) in Baltimore. However, it wasn't a good interview; the INS officer asked me for specific dates and details regarding particular incidents, but I was still suffering from sleeplessness and couldn't reply to her satisfaction. As I walked out of the INS office, I knew I would not be granted asylum.

Although Hodan was disappointed, she understood that I wasn't feeling well and that the timing of the interview couldn't have been worse. Allan Ebert was not aware of my sleep deprivation and was quite dismayed with my performance.

I decided that the only thing to do was to start looking for a job. I began sending out resumes but couldn't get a position that related to my studies. If I'd had the luxury of looking for a job over a period of two or three months, probably I could have gotten a suitable job related to my degree, but it was urgent for me to earn a living. I started to work as a security guard, sometimes guarding malls and private businesses and at other times guarding government offices.

I didn't like the work at all and didn't feel useful. I felt that I had fallen from grace. I even became nostalgic for the good old days in Somalia, when I had been the director of a department and had a car and a driver. I had earned a graduate degree from one of the best universities in the USA. Yet all that had come to naught. Moreover, I was working the night shift, which did not sit well with my history of sleeplessness.

Hodan, meanwhile, worked at a clerical job at Georgetown University while searching for a full-time professional position. Nevertheless we decided it was time to get married. On March 27, 1990, we became engaged and got married soon after. Our son Mohamed was born on the same date exactly one year later. I continued working as a security guard and Hodan continued her clerical job, but now with the added responsibility of a child to support. Little more than a year later, on July 28, 1992, our second son, Ahmed, was born. Life was not easy, but I enjoyed my family life.

Still, I wanted to continue pursuing a Ph.D. I had fully withdrawn from the University of Connecticut at Storrs but had received admission from George Mason University (GMU), in Fairfax, Virginia. GMU said it would admit me in the fall of 1992, but did not offer financial assistance. Fortunately, as a resident of Virginia I had in-state tuition, which was not as expensive as out-of-state tuition. I started with a part-time schedule, taking two courses per semester rather than the full load of three or more per semester.

But one problem remained: my school schedule conflicted with my work as a security guard, and my employer refused to accommodate the schedule. Hodan had a 9-to-5 job, and her work schedule was quite restrictive. Some friends told me that I could make more money driving a cab than as a security guard and that I could set my own schedule, driving a cab in the morning and attending school in the afternoon. GMU's graduate program catered to full-time professional workers, and as a result most of my graduate courses were scheduled for either late afternoons or evenings. Cab driving gave me the flexibility to attend classes while taking care of my boys.

For almost a year I took care of Ahmed during the day, went to school in the afternoon, and drove the cab in late evenings. After the first three semesters at GMU I was offered a Bradley fellowship, which covered my tuition and paid $15,000 for my living expenses. I was able to quit driving a cab and to study full time. I am grateful to Professor Walter E. Williams for providing me with this timely fellowship. It came at an opportune time in my life, and I am forever grateful.

I was, however, still waiting for the INS to respond to my bid for political asylum. But nothing came, just silence. I sent inquiry letters almost every week, and the response was always the same: "Your case is still pending. We will let you know when we have more information." I became frustrated.

Finally, Hodan, who had already been granted asylum, suggested that I apply through her, based on our marriage. I accepted the situation and we filed all the paperwork. The response was immediate; in March 1994, the INS instructed me to leave the country to get approval. The usual INS procedure was that anyone applying through reunion or through marriage should leave the United States, return to their native country, and receive approval in that country.

There was a dilemma here: I couldn't return to Somalia because it was at the height of its civil war. My lawyer briefed the INS about the situation, so the INS instructed me to go to Mexico and receive approval there instead. In May 1994, I traveled to Ciudad Juarez, Mexico, across the border from El Paso, Texas, and was given an advance parole—a one-time exit and reentry permit—which allowed me to leave the United States and reenter legally only once. I presented all my documentation to the U.S. consulate in Ciudad Juarez. However, although all the documentation had been previously submitted and approved, the agent looked at my passport and saw that I had left the United States in October 1988 and returned in June 1989—I hadn't stayed in Somalia for two years, as required by my J1 visa. My application was immediately rejected.

I tried to reason with the agent, explaining that I had returned legally on a G2 visa and had no country to return to. Instead of considering my unique circumstance, he said: "Sir, will you remove yourself from my window." Two muscular marines grabbed me by the shoulders, lifted me up, and threw me out of the consulate compound. This was one of the lowest moments in my life: no response to my asylum application, and now this. It felt like the sky was falling on me and that the whole world had turned against me.

I returned to Washington empty-handed. Hodan and I went back to Allan Ebert, who said, "The INS has no case. We will take the INS and U.S. Department of Justice to court." We sued the government, stating that I could not return to Somalia, that there was no government there, and the civil war was at its height. I had been in the United States on the basis of valid documentation; I had a wife and American-born children living there; and I was a law-abiding citizen pursuing a graduate degree in the country.

We were given a court date, but less than a week before that date I received a letter indicating that I had been granted asylum. The INS decided it was not worth its time and money to take me to court. This letter gave me another perspective on America and the American justice system: an immigrant from Somalia could sue the United States government, the Justice Department in particular and win!

The Civil War in Somalia

Though I was now living in the United States, I remained concerned about the political situation in Somalia. I supported the guerrilla movement against the Siad Barre regime and believed that there was a need for regime change. That this change would involve the clans in Somalia was inescapable. Somalis are categorized into four main clans: the Dir, Darod, Hawiye, and Digil and Mirifle, and it was commonly accepted that there was a clan "dimension to all the opposition movements. Besides the Majertein-based SSDF and Isaaq-based SNM groups, both operating out of Ethiopia, in 1989 a new armed opposition group, the United Somali Congress (USC), had been formed in Rome by former politicians and businessmen hailing from the Hawiye clan of central Somalia.

However, it never occurred to me these groups would be as short-sighted as they turned out to be. Not in my wildest imaginings did I think they would turn their guns on the same people who had supported them a few months earlier. Some of the opposition groups had ulterior motives. The SNM wanted to dismember the country and had a secessionist agenda. On May 18, 1991, it declared in Burao that the north had seceded from Somalia. The south, meanwhile, had descended into a multi-faceted civil war characterized by large-scale atrocities. Thus, all of a sudden Somalis went from being enthusiastic about Siad Barre's downfall to disillusionment. We went from elation into survival mode.

The USC was interested not only in deposing Siad Barre, but also in eliminating the whole Darod clan family, which it perceived as its mortal enemy. Most Darod civilians were totally taken by surprise when they suddenly felt an existential threat not only from the Hawiye clan but also from those who resented the perceived privileges enjoyed by some segments of the Darod clan family. The USC went into genocidal mode and began a "clan cleansing" of the Darods.

A few days after Siad Barre left Mogadishu, grim news emerged of the massacre. Hundreds if not thousands of prominent Darods had been killed in cold blood by marauding USC militia in Mogadishu. It was now clear that the USC was not just against Siad Barre many of whose leading henchmen were amongst its members, but also in favor of cleansing the Darods from Mogadishu and large parts of central and south-central Somalia. This was a disaster in the making: thousands of war-torn refugees and internally displaced people were starving to death every day.

In the United States, Somalis who were united against the Siad Barre regime quickly became polarized. The clan fissures in Somalia were reflected in the behavior of Somalis in the USA: Darod versus Hawiye, and the Digil and Mirifle in between. Friends who had been unified against Siad Barre a month or two earlier now could not see eye to eye.

As the first batch of Somali refugees escaped and began to arrive in the United States, they told horror stories of children being dismembered, young men being killed, and young women being raped. Somalis pleaded to the United Nations to intervene and continuously wrote to UN Secretary General Boutros Boutros-Ghali. A number of Somalis in the United States—including myself, Abdullahi Farah Holif, and Abdullahi Mohamoud Hassan (Matukade)—made the rounds in Washington, asking Congress and the State Department to address the deteriorating situation in Somalia and, if necessary, to intervene militarily to safeguard the little that remained of the Somali nation.

In addition to the brewing civil war, extreme drought struck the breadbasket of Somalia. It was becoming clear that it would be morally repugnant not to intervene. Faced with a humanitarian disaster that was exacerbated by a complete breakdown of law and civil order, President George H.W. Bush announced that the United States would intervene and authorized a large contingent of U.S. Marines to be deployed in Somalia. Subsequently, on December 3, 1992, the UN Security Council unanimously adopted Resolution 794 authorizing the use of all necessary means to establish a secure environment for humanitarian relief operations in Somalia. Soon afterward, on December 9, the U.S. Marines landed on the beaches of Mogadishu.

The initial reaction in the United States was very positive. The

U.S. government was providing relief to people who were suffering from both anarchy and drought. Operation Restore Hope, as it was called, was a very successful show of force that brought the killing of innocent Somalis and the extortion of aid agencies to an end. In the meantime, however, General Mohamed Farah Aideed, the most powerful warlord in Mogadishu, defied UN Security Council resolutions and demanded the withdrawal of peacekeepers, as well as declaring hostilities against all UN deployments.

On October 3, 1993, the infamous Black Hawk Down incident occurred, in which two American helicopters were shot down by Aideed's forces. Eighteen U.S. Marines were killed, as were an untold number of Somali civilians and combatants. The bodies of U.S. Marines were dragged through the streets of Mogadishu. When the U.S. public saw the people they were feeding were dragging Americans through the streets of Mogadishu, the political tide turned. Public reaction to Black Hawk Down forced President Bill Clinton, who had succeeded George H.W. Bush as president in January 1993, to withdraw U.S. forces from Somalia.

Completing My Studies in America

During this period of anarchy in Somalia, the Darod clan had not been militarily defeated and chased out of Mogadishu; rather, most of its members, unwilling to fight for the notorious regime, had left the city of their own volition. They inched toward Afgooye, then Marka, then Kismayo, and ultimately found themselves near the border with Kenya. Now the dominant clan in Mogadishu was the Hawiye, where before the numbers of Darod and Hawiye clan members had been fairly even.

I was concerned about the whereabouts of my family, who had left Dusamareb as the country collapsed into clan warfare and traveled to Galkayo. They had been unable to contact us because, outside of Mogadishu and a few other towns, Somalia had no telephone communication systems. After months of confusion, my aunt traveled from Galkayo to Diridawa, Ethiopia, so that she could telephone us. Some of my other relatives who were residing in Mogadishu before the war broke out had made it to refugee camps in Kenya. They had access to telephones there and were able to call us.

This was a time of constant worry for me. I was attending school part time in the early 1990s, and it took me seven years to finish my Ph.D. In 1997, I finished the coursework and submitted my dissertation proposal for approval. The dissertation committee accepted my proposal and recommended that I proceed with writing my dissertation. In the meantime, I received a fellowship from Harvard University. I went to Harvard in 1998, where I was enrolled in the International Tax Program (ITP) at the law school while pursuing a master's in public administration at the Kennedy School of Government. A fellowship covered my tuition at Harvard, after which the Kennedy School gave me a teaching fellowship for living expenses.

I assisted professors George Borjas and David Ellwood in reviewing and grading economics courses, for which I received a modest stipend of $1,200. It seems the students liked my lectures and gave me good reviews, because one day Professor Borjas summoned me to his office. "Mr. Ali," he said, "you have doubled the demand, so we will double the supply." He would double my salary and give me double the number of students to teach.

This was welcome news, because by then Hodan had started her Ph.D. studies at George Mason University, in the same program in which I was enrolled, and there we had another child: our daughter Fadumo was born on April 29, 1998. Hodan was on maternity leave but had a full-time job at Georgetown University. In addition, I was an adjunct professor of economics at Northern Virginia Community College from 1993 until 1998. I left for Harvard just a little over a month after Fadumo was born, and by that time Hodan was finishing her coursework. It was good for us that Hodan joined me in the same program, as I was able to tutor her. Every other weekend, I traveled from Boston to Virginia to visit her and the children.

I also became an armchair politician in the 1990s, as a large number of Somalis arrived in the United States in the early part of the decade. For people who had lost their country and were once in refugee camps in Kenya, it was a blessing to be able to come to America. I was asked to appear on interview programs on Channel 4 and Channel 8 in the Washington area as a Somali analyst. It was a busy time for all of us.

From the Commonwealth of Virginia to Niagara University

After graduating from George Mason University in January 2000, I joined the state government of the Commonwealth of Virginia as a research and forecast manager. It was a fast-paced, high-paying job, and also stressful. The Virginia constitution stipulates that the state cannot incur any expenditure without a proper forecast; basically, the state budget was based on the forecast. Virginia, a relatively wealthy state, had an annual budget in the billions of dollars. Thus, a forecast error of 1 or 2 percent could translate into the hundreds of millions of dollars. As a member of the Technical Forecast Committee, I was designated to forecast the expenditure on corrections.

The committee reported its findings to the politicians, a group not usually enamored with forecasts based on complicated models. Often they do not understand why forecasting models might sometimes be off the mark and cannot accept that errors might be made. A forecast error of 2 percent might mean that fewer schools or prisons would be built. These were (and remain) politically sensitive issues that could cost politicians elections.

I performed this work diligently for three years. In the forecast season, I left for work at 6:30 in the morning, when the children were still asleep, and returned at 10 in the evening, when they were in bed. Work took over; I needed a beeper and a cell phone, and to be ready to be called in to work at any moment. This was in stark contrast to my previous job at Virginia Community College, where I had enjoyed the academic environment and had fallen in love with teaching.

When the Virginia state job became overly stressful, I decided to return to academia and look for a teaching position. In January 2003, I attended the American Economic Association Conference in Washington to explore the possibility of finding a suitable position. I set up a series of interviews with various universities and, just as I was becoming exhausted, noticed two gentlemen sitting at a table that sported a sign indicating they were from Niagara University. Although I had no appointment, I walked up to them and asked about the university, which I discovered was located in Lewiston, New York, near Buffalo. The two men were economists Phillip Scherer and Stan Warren, who had come to Washington to hire an economics professor. We started a conversation and immediately found common ground. Phil Scherer and I had the same political outlook and philosophy. I had already published half a dozen articles in refereed journals, so we happily discussed the collapse of communism, the downfall of the Soviet Union, and how the market economy had won, among other subjects.

Phil and Stan invited me to visit Niagara University in March. The weather was very discouraging. At first I was not impressed, as Lewiston was too cold for my comfort and the flight from Richmond, Virginia, to Buffalo was cancelled twice because the runway was too icy. However, when I arrived in Lewiston, the beauty of the campus and the warmth of the people at the business school impressed me tremendously. Niagara University, a Catholic school with an excellent academic reputation, is relatively small, with a student population of four thousand students. It is one of three U.S. universities in the Vincentian tradition, following the teachings of Saint Vincent De Paul—the other two are De Paul University in Chicago and St. John's University in New York. The Vincentian philosophy is based on helping the poor, a perspective that resonated with me, a citizen of a poor country like Somalia.

I liked the environment, the people, and the professors I met at Niagara University, and I accepted the offer to teach there. I had also received an offer from the American University of Sharjah, in the United Arab Emirates, but I chose Niagara for two reasons. First, I wanted to excel as an academic, and the research facilities and support at Niagara were much better. Niagara had a rigorous tenure system that also required publishing. This requirement would push me to excel in my research as well as to increase my knowledge. Second, the American University in Sharjah didn't have a good retirement or benefits system. For a man with a family, this was important. Life might have been more fun if I had gone to Dubai, but it would not have been more rewarding. I started teaching at Niagara in August. Dean Jack Helmuth, also an economist, was very supportive and made my transition as easy as possible.

Two weeks after my arrival at Niagara University, we had a new addition to our family. On September 8, 2003, our third son, Mustafa Abdiweli, was born in Richmond, Virginia. For the next few years, I continued to teach at Niagara and to spend time with my young family. Throughout my time at Niagara I continued my engagement with Somalia, and in the summer of 2008 I traveled to Puntland, Somalia, to teach at Puntland State University. I wanted to give back to my country, which had given me a free education. Not only did I want to use my summer vacation to teach; I was eager to share what I had learned in the United States.

In 2010, I decided to take a complete year of sabbatical from teaching at Niagara and looked into the possibilities of teaching and doing research at other institutions. As I was contemplating another offer, I received a call from the Qualified Expatriate Somali Technical Support–Migration for Development in Africa (QUESTS–MIDA) program to spend a year in Somalia as a consultant on public finance.

Flanked by Augustine Mahiga (right), the Prime Minister of the Transitional Federal Government of Somalia, Abdiweli Mohamed Ali (centre), addresses correspondents following a Security Council meeting September 2011 United Nations, New York UN Photo/Rick Bajornas

Garowe Two (II) Conference February 18, 2012 Garowe, Puntland, Somalia

The stipend was not as attractive as the one in the offer I was considering, but I thought: If you are going to a desert, why not go to the one where you really belong? And, having a nomadic background, I was longing for camel's milk. I decided to return to Somalia, under the QUEST–MIDA program, to help the Puntland Ministry of Finance with public finance management, especially taxation and revenue generation. Once again I would be able to share what I had learned and perhaps put it to good use.

RETURN TO SOMALIA:

THE TRANSITIONAL FEDERAL GOVERMENT AND THE KAMPALA ACCORD

The Joint Needs Assessment Project

I had always followed Somali politics, sometimes from afar—as when I was an armchair politician in Washington in the 1990s—and sometimes more closely. There were also times, before returning to Somalia in 2010, when I was more actively engaged. In late 2005 and early 2006, during the tenure of President Abdullahi Yusuf and Prime Minister Ali Mohamed Ghedi, I had been among a group of experts tasked to formulate a reconstruction and development plan for Somalia. We were hired by the United Nations Development Program (UNDP) and the World Bank to work on a joint needs assessment (JNA) project for Somalia. I was one of the lead persons in the macroeconomic cluster particularly assigned to work on fiscal policy issues because of my academic background and professional experience in tax policy and revenue analysis.

Based in Nairobi, we paid extensive visits to Somalia, visiting Somaliland, Puntland, Beledwein, Baidoa, and Jowhar, at that time the seat of Somalia's Transitional Federal Government (TFG). I was struck by how much Somalia, particularly Puntland, had changed over the decades. The landscape was drastically different. Due to the influx of people who had fled the war in the south, cities in Puntland had grown immensely. Galkayo, for example, was now a cosmopolitan city with modern restaurants, hotels, and shopping centers.

There had been an exorbitant and agonizing increase in the price of commodities. In 2000, the exchange rate for one U.S. dollar had been 16,000 Somali shillings. Now, in 2006, it was double that rate. By 2000, more than a million people had left Somalia to seek safety in Western Europe, Canada, the United States, and Australia, and as a result huge remittances were being sent to Somalia from the diaspora community overseas. This mitigated the situation in Somalia to some extent, and life was not as difficult as it might have been.

Somalis once had a government, functioning schools, and fully operational hospitals. They had aspired to a better future, which they believed was within their reach if they worked hard. Now they felt hopeless. The light at the end of the tunnel had been effectively extinguished by the lack of governing institutions and senseless civil strife. Young people were not as idealistic and optimistic as they had once been. They fully understood their situation and the harsh realities of Somalia: there was no functioning government—national, regional, or otherwise.

Fewer than 15 percent of school-age girls and only about 20 percent of school-age boys were attending school, whereas a few decades earlier 80 percent of school-age children were attending classes. No doubt this was due to the fact that those who lived in a city with schools received free instruction. Now it was a completely different situation. The vacuum created by the absence of a functioning state was being filled by the private sector and local non-governmental organizations. Established schools and clinics provided other social services, but the need was much greater than they could satisfy. Education was out of reach for children from poor families. Furthermore, there was little incentive to learn: children might go to school and graduate, but then they faced a dismal future. There would in all likelihood be no job, no career, and no income for them. They would remain unemployed and hopeless.

The JNA study was a very good and timely program, and we put together a comprehensive document that entailed a massive collection of data throughout the country. It was one of the best studies done to date in Somalia, covering all aspects of the country's social, economic, and political spheres. It was categorized into six clusters—macroeconomics, social services, livelihood, rule of law and security, production, and infrastructure—with further sub-clusters and cross-cutting issues. Unfortunately, due to the absence of a stable political environment in Somalia, the study's findings and recommendations have not yet been utilized. When the situation improves, this project's data will be put to good use I hope.

My Arrival in Mogadishu

After returning to Puntland from the United States in July 2010, I began my consulting work at the Ministry of Finance. My duties and immediate future seemed straightforward and predictable. However, in October I received a call from Mohamed Farmajo, who had been appointed the prime minister of Somalia on October 14 but hadn't yet been confirmed by the Parliament. He asked me to join the government of Somalia in Mogadishu. At first I was reluctant, not only because of the security situation in Mogadishu, but also, more importantly, because Somalia's Transitional Federal Government (TFG) was considered to have bad leadership. The TFG had been weakened by constant squabbling among the higher echelons of the government.

I asked the prime minister to give me a couple of days to discuss this with Hodan and my family. Farmajo, however, called me again the next day to ask me to be his deputy, with the added position of minister of planning and international cooperation. Thinking this would be an opportunity for me to serve the country in a larger capacity, I decided to accept the offer to become Somalia's deputy prime minister and minister of planning and international cooperation. I contacted QUESTS–MIDA to inform them that I would be joining Somalia's new cabinet. The timing was good, as the TFG's mandate would expire on August 20, 2011, and my sabbatical year from Niagara University would also end in that month. It was a perfect fit.

I arrived in Mogadishu on November 21, 2010. The state of the city was a shock to me. Once a peaceful city—almost a seaside resort, with beautiful beaches frequented by elegant and stylish people—the capital had been gutted by the civil war. Everywhere one looked, there were dilapidated buildings occupied by internally displaced people. The government controlled less than half the city; the terrorist organization al-Shabaab, al-Qaeda's franchise in Somalia, controlled the rest. Gun-toting youngsters were strolling about everywhere, likewise, some members of the Somali National Army and others belonging to private militias were ubiquitously seen.

At first I wondered what I had got myself into. Prime Minister Farmajo had appointed a technocratic and competent cabinet, but the approval process was complicated by the fact that the speaker of Parliament, Sharif Hassan Sheikh Aden, had had a falling-out with President Sheikh Sharif. Eventually, with much arm-twisting and coaxing of the members of Parliament, the new cabinet was approved on November 28.

The task of reconstruction seemed overwhelming: how could we do meaningful work in this badly damaged city and country? I was immediately taken to the Sahafi Hotel, one of the most secure hotels in Mogadishu. After getting settled, I went to Villa Somalia to visit the prime minister. It was a daunting task, but Prime Minister Farmajo had a positive personality. He was optimistic and willing to take all the necessary risks. He took me to meet President Sheikh Sharif a couple of days later. I had never met Sheikh Sharif before and felt that he was too young and inexperienced to be the president of a broken country. He didn't look quite "presidential" to me. But when we sat down and discussed the issues of government, he was very cordial, well-spoken, and smart. He was very enthusiastic about the new prime minister and the new cabinet.

Sheikh Sharif had become the head of the Islamic Courts Union (ICU), a group of clan courts based in Mogadishu, in 2006. This system of sharia-based Islamic courts had become Somalia's main judicial system, funded through fees paid by the litigants, after the collapse of the Somali state in 1991. Over time, the courts had begun to offer other services, such as education and healthcare. Although almost every clan had established its own courts, they soon saw the sense in working together through a joint committee to promote security and formed one to coordinate their affairs, to exchange criminals among different clans for the purposes of justice, and to integrate security forces.

Around the time Sheikh Sharif was chosen to head the ICU, the U.S. Central Intelligence Agency (CIA) made a disingenuous deal with Somali warlords to support them in fighting "extremist elements" in Somalia. The warlords at that time had a stranglehold on Somalia, particularly on the inhabitants of Mogadishu. The people of Mogadishu hated these warlords; nevertheless, the CIA funded the warlords' alliance instead of supporting the TFG, the legitimate government of Somalia. Not surprisingly, the ICU felt threatened and reacted violently against the warlords. When fighting broke out between these groups, most residents of Mogadishu sided with the ICU and lent it their moral and material support.

Although the warlords were armed with the benefit of millions of dollars from the CIA, they were no match for the will of the people. They were quickly defeated and chased out of Mogadishu. Some of them fled to Ethiopia, while others ran to their clan strongholds and fled as far away as Congo. But the ICU pursued them and chased them out of their hideouts. Finally, the fugitive warlords sought the protection of the TFG, the same government they had vehemently opposed only a few months earlier. Ironically, a number of them had been government ministers, and as a result the TFG, being a government of reconciliation, could not turn them away. Instead, the TFG leaders decided to cajole them and convince them to cooperate. What the TFG had not been able to accomplish earlier was ultimately been done for it by the ICU: the warlords had to either leave the country or join the TFG. Unfortunately elements of the ICU threatened and provoked the TFG headquartered in Baidao and the Ethiopian intervention that followed led to many human rights violations against ordinary people and contributed to the strengthening of what came to be known as Al Shabaab.

Reorganizing the Ministry of Planning

In the midst of this national turmoil, on my appointment as Somalia's deputy prime minister and minister of planning and international cooperation, I immediately set to work. On my first day at the Ministry of Planning, I was taken to the office of the minister who had preceded me. I turned on his computer, and there was not a single file visible in it. I had nothing to work with; there was absolutely no documentation to guide me through the process. There was no Internet connection, and thus no possibility of doing any meaningful work. I could only find hard copies of some ministry documents here and there.

The bureaucracy, too, was completely dysfunctional. Three different men claimed to be the director general, although only one—Nur Weheliye, the oldest of them and a true gentleman—was suitable in terms of credentials and demeanor. The ministry employees were very diligent, but they were working under very difficult circumstances, not only in terms of livelihood—they were not being paid regularly—but also because of the lack of security. By the time I arrived, they had been paid perhaps only two or three times in the past two years. Furthermore, they were targeted by al-Shabaab because they were considered apostates who were aiding and abetting the infidels. Ministry employees were facing a constant threat—some had even been assassinated—and they were demoralized by their superiors' lack of empathy and the lack of support from the government they had sacrificed so much for. As a result, they often quarreled, and the work environment was somewhat toxic when I arrived.

Knowing that it was important to immediately start paying our employees, allaying their fears, and assuaging their cynicism about the government, I decided to appoint a new director general and restructure the ministry. I needed assistance, so I asked the UNDP for help. It responded positively—particularly Alvaro Rodriguez, the head of the UNDP at the time. He was well aware of the state of the ministry and was very supportive of my efforts.

I brought in a new director general, Abdullahi Sheikh, from

Nairobi. Abdullahi had been the director of the technical department in the Ministry of Planning of Somalia in the 1980s. He had a good record with the ministry and a wealth of experience in planning and international cooperation. His appointment changed the environment at the ministry, and soon a completely different atmosphere developed. Two of the fighting trio of previous director generals left the ministry, and Nur Weheliye stayed on to work in a different capacity.

Thus, I succeeded in reshaping the ministry: there was a new division of labor, a renewed organizational structure, a change in the top bureaucratic leadership, and a resumption of payments to employees. The employees, not surprisingly, became enthusiastic about their work. Some of those who had left the ministry long before I arrived returned when they heard the good news. By the time I left the ministry, it had leadership and it was functional, with computers, printers, and Internet. In the seven months that I was minister of planning, it became a completely different institution.

The Kampala Accord

The speaker of the house, Shariff Hassan Sheikh Aden, and President Sheikh Sharif had once been very close friends. No one knows why they had a falling-out, but the conflict between the two manifested itself politically because one was the head of the legislative branch of the TFG and the other was the head of the executive. This resulted in political infighting in which each leader was eager to oust the other.

Prime Minister Farmajo was caught in the middle but decided to side with Sheikh Sharif. He felt that Shariff Hassan Sheikh Aden was mischievous and harbored sinister motives against his government. At the same time, Abdirahman Mohamed Farole, the president of Puntland, had a difficult time in engaging with both Farmajo and Sheikh Sharif. Farole felt there was an anti-Puntland drive by the TFG and that the TFG was not supportive enough of Puntland's autonomy as a federal state. He was abrasive and confrontational, and the distrust was mutual: Sheikh Sharif and Farmajo didn't like Farole either. Farole was very much against the appointment of Farmajo as prime minister, and this created a wedge between the

TFG and Puntland. He made a deal with Shariff Hassan, the speaker. President Caalin of Galmudug also felt that Sheikh Sharif was supporting the man who was vying with him for the presidency of Galmudug.

In the midst of this infighting, the TFG mandate was set to expire in a few months, on August 20, 2011. On April 13, with Galmudug and Puntland states at odds with the TFG, Shariff Hassan, Farole, and Caalin met in Nairobi under the auspices of United Nations Political Office for Somalia (UNPOS) to deal with the conflicts. Sheikh Sharif refused to attend the conference, creating a schism between Ambassador Augustine Mahiga, the UN Secretary General's Representative for Somalia, and the leadership of Somalia. There Shariff Hassan, Farole, and Caalin released a joint communiqué calling for the extension of the term of the TFG Parliament by two years. UNPOS, with its mandate to supervise the direction of Somalia's political regime, hosted the conference in Nairobi and supported the outcome of the conference.

Parliament received a new lease on life from this meeting in Nairobi: an extension of its mandate necessitated a new government. The unilateral extension of the term of Parliament was a knee-jerk response to President Sheikh Sharif and Prime Minister Farmajo. This is what Shariff Hassan had wanted as the outcome of the conference: to remain as the speaker of Parliament but to be rid of Sheikh Sharif and Farmajo.

Upon returning to Somalia, Shariff Hassan called on Parliament to endorse the outcome of the Nairobi conference. Parliament held an extraordinary session and instead extended its term not just by two years, as agreed in Nairobi, but by three years, which would make August 2014 the end of its term. Not surprisingly, there was uproar about the audacity of this unilateral extension of its mandate. It was claimed that the unilateral extension of the term was not only justified by the federal charter but also in the interest of Somalia—it would avoid a political vacuum, as the TFG's term was about to end. This was self-justifying, as Parliament had neither the right nor the power to unilaterally extend its own mandate.

On June 2–3, the International Contact Group (ICG) on Somalia held a conference in Kampala. Members of the ICG noted that

Somalis must reach an agreement on the transition, and, if there were to be an extension, it would be for no more than twelve months, ending in August 2012, for all TFG institutions unless circumstances dictated otherwise. After long deliberations, the ICG decided that the TFG's mandate would be extended for both Parliament and the executive branch of the government, including the president, for only one year. This one-year extension was eventually won with the help of Uganda, Djibouti, and other friendly countries.

This was a victory for the president and the prime minister, for two reasons. First, in limiting the extension to one year for both Parliament and the cabinet, the ICG's decision was contrary to the unilateral decision of the Somali Federal Parliament and its leader Shariff Hassan Sheikh Aden. Second, the extension was an acknowledgment by the international community of the exceptional performance of the cabinet. It constituted an approval of the accomplishments of the prime minister and the cabinet and an encouragement to continue the fight against al-Shabaab. It gave the cabinet a clean bill of health and sanctioned the fact that the cabinet should be given time to finish its work.

The ICG's decision was final. This was the result the executive branch had wanted. It was a defeat for Shariff Hassan and all those who had colluded against the TFG in Nairobi. As a result, Shariff Hassan was forced to swallow the decision and to work with Sheikh Sharif and Farmajo for another year.

Given the new situation, Ambassador Mahiga, under the auspices of UNPOS, sought to bridge the gap between Sheikh Sharif and Shariff Hassan, with the tutelage of President Yoweri Museveni of Uganda. Somehow in Kampala, under Mahiga, the two men made a deal without the consent of the rest of the delegates, entailing the resignation of Prime Minister Farmajo. This conspiratorial agreement was supported by both Museveni and Mahiga, who were desperately seeking a way out of the impasse. The political stalemate negatively impacted not only the performance of the TFG and the fight against al-Shabaab, but also that of the Ugandan troops who were risking life and limb to save Somalia from anarchy.

The question arose, how could the deal have been done? On the one hand, Mahiga and Museveni spoke neither Arabic nor

Somali. On the other hand, Shariff Hassan and Sheikh Sharif had no command of the English language. Yet, miraculously, the four men met and finalized a deal. No one knows how. I later asked Sheikh Sharif how in the world they had communicated with Mahiga and Museveni. He said, "If you add the little that Shariff Hassan knows and the little I know about English, it worked out."

Just before the ICG conference in Kampala, I had returned from an overseas trip to Turkey. I had a lot of catching up to do and tried to excuse myself from the delegation, but Prime Minister Farmajo insisted that I accompany the president to the conference. I reluctantly accepted after he pleaded that it was important to have TFG cabinet members at that important meeting. Three ministers attended as part of the president's delegation: Minister of Education Dr. Abdinur Sheikh Mohamud, Minister of Information and Telecommunication Abdikarim Hassan Jama, and myself.

When we came to understand what was occurring behind closed doors, Abdinur and I took a walk around the Munyoyo resort where the delegation was staying to discuss our options. We did not include Abdikarim Hassan Jama in our walk because we felt he was too close to the president. We said a prayer to Allah to give us guidance and decided that we could not be part of this conspiracy. We had no choice but to resign. We felt that the deal between Sheikh Sharif and Shariff Hassan was unjust and unwarranted, and merely served the personal and parochial interests of the two men. Abdinur and I believed that the prime minister had been unfairly treated and that the deal was deceitful in its treatment not only of Farmajo, but also of the whole cabinet. We wrote our resignation letters and as cabinet members had to submit them to the prime minister before taking them to the president. We called Mogadishu and told Farmajo what had happened in Kampala, as news of the deal hadn't yet reached Mogadishu.

Farmajo refused to accept our resignation. He said he was coming to Kampala and asked us not to act precipitously. He flew to Kampala the next day, on June 7, arriving at approximately 1 a.m. We had our resignation letters ready, but when he arrived he said, "Take me to the president." Sheikh Sharif was aware that Farmajo was coming, and he was waiting for the prime minister. By now it was 2 a.m., and because of the continuous commotion of the last two days Abdinur and I were exhausted. We retired to our rooms, expecting Farmajo to brief us in the morning after his meeting with the president.

Abdinur and I were having breakfast the following morning when I was told that President Sheikh Sharif wanted to see me. When I got there, he, Prime Minister Farmajo, and Abdikarim, the information minister, were waiting for me. I was told that Farmajo had decided to resign on the condition that I would agree to be the next prime minister. I was astounded for a moment. I asked the prime minister, "Do you agree with this? Are you comfortable with this decision?" Farmajo answered, "Yes." I asked again: "Have you really, really thought about it? Are you having any second thoughts?" I wanted him to say, even once, "Maybe I do have second thoughts about this."

Farmajo's elder brother Salah, who was waiting outside the room, was suspicious of what was going on in inside. I suggested that we have the courtesy to tell him about the prime minister's decision to resign. Mohamed Farmajo refused because, he said, his brother would not accept this turn of events. He said, "Don't worry. I will break the news to him. Let's just go ahead." Later on, his brother did in fact take the news badly.

There was no guarantee that events would go ahead as agreed. We never knew whether, even if Farmajo resigned, Sheikh Sharif would honor the agreement to appoint me as prime minister. In addition, the appointment had to be approved by Parliament, and Shariff Hassan also had to be in agreement. Still uncertain about these surprising turns of events, the president, the prime minister and I made a religious oath on the Qur'an that I would accept the offer, that Farmajo would resign, and that Sheikh Sharif would keep his word. This was a secret deal between us, which we did not make public.

Shariff Hassan traveled to Nairobi the next day, and Farmajo, Sheikh Sharif, and the rest of the delegation returned to Mogadishu. I stayed behind for the funeral of a Ugandan colonel who had been killed in Mogadishu in an AMISOM operation, and I then flew to Liberia to attend a conference on fragile states. Although I was not in Somalia, I was the presumptive nominee for prime minister. But there was work to be done there, and there were obstacles along the way: Parliament had to accept what was now known as the Kampala Accord. First, it had to accept Farmajo's resignation as prime minister. Then, the president had to convince Parliament to vote for me as prime minister. This was not an easy task, as the rapport between Parliament and Farmajo was not particularly great, and Parliament was also against the agreement to reduce the unilateral extension of its term to just one year. The members were annoyed that there had been a secret deal between Sheikh Sharif and Shariff Hassan, in effect saying: "What's the point of getting rid of Farmajo and replacing him with his deputy, who is very close to him?" The president had a lot of convincing to do.

A further complication set in: Farmajo became convinced that his decision had been wrong, and now he refused to resign as prime minister. There were resulting riots in support of Farmajo and against Sheikh Sharif and Shariff Hassan. The public was not aware that a secret deal—that I would take over—had been made. If they had known that I would be the next prime minister, this knowledge might have prevented some of the riots. These riots emboldened Farmajo and some ministers, and various cabinet members and other members of Parliament advised Farmajo not to step down.

Progress in carrying out the terms of the Kampala Accord was coming to a screeching halt, so a delegation traveled from Uganda to Mogadishu to convince Farmajo to resign. The Ugandan contingent was responsible for the security of the president and the prime minister, and their future in Somalia was at stake. It threw its weight behind the Kampala Accord, and once again the prime minister

agreed to resign. He finally did so on June 19.

The president appointed me as prime minister of the TFG on June 23. On June 28, Parliament almost unanimously approved my nomination, with 437 members voting "yes" and two members voting "no," with only four abstentions. Many members of Parliament were aware of my independent streak, and I believe they welcomed my appointment.

We showed our appreciation to Mohamed Farmajo by holding a farewell party for the former prime minister. He left in good standing with the Somali people. He will be remembered as a prime minister with vision; he had only seven months to make a difference to the nation, and made remarkable progress. One of the most important achievements during his tenure was ensuring that civil servants and the military were paid regularly. This boosted their morale tremendously—not a small feat in a broken country.

CREATING A GOVERNMENT:

CABINET MAKING AND GOVERNING IN A TIME OF FAMINE

Forming a Cabinet

My first task after having been confirmed as prime minister was to inform Parliament of my political program and my agenda for taking Somalia forward. I intended to be a unifying leader and to take on the role of mediator, and facilitator. In an effort to put the members of Parliament at ease, I promised to regularly consult with them and to do whatever I could to remove the discord between the legislative and the executive branches of the government. Their working relationship was at its lowest point, so improving that relationship was of paramount importance. I pledged that I would select a committed cabinet, and that together we would fight al-Shabaab and establish an institutional framework to guide the country politically, socially, and economically.

I had a thirty-day window from the time I was appointed on June 23 to form a cabinet and submit the year-long program of my government to Parliament. Earlier, as a member of Farmajo's cabinet, I had developed a close relationship with the other members of that cabinet. We were a close-knit group, and I was familiar with the special talents of each minister. My intention was to keep the majority of my colleagues as members of the new government, both because of their earlier notable performance and for the sake of continuity in government.

I needed to meet with the president of the TFG, Sheikh Sharif Sheikh Ahmed, as it was his prerogative to approve the cabinet I had appointed. When I visited him to discuss the formation of the government, he said: "We will be joined by the speaker, Shariff Hassan Sheikh Aden." I asked him why this was necessary, because I felt there was no role for the speaker in this process. He said, "This is how things have been done since Abdullahi Yusuf's time—a consultation between the prime minister, the speaker, and the president." I had the impression that the speaker was transgressing his legislative powers and that the president was being too accommodating of him. Someone had to rein in the undue influence of the speaker.

The Kampala Accord was problematic here because it had given a role to the speaker. Article 4(g) of the Accord stipulates that cabinet appointments will be made "in the spirit of collaboration and mutual confidence between the leaders of the TFIs in accordance with their respective mandates." Although there is no specific mandate here for the speaker, he had somehow become part of the process since Abdullahi's term as president. This precedent interfered with the system of governance. I resisted it as much as I could, knowing the speaker was not fond of the former prime minister and his cabinet. Neither did he share my desire to keep the majority of the members of the previous cabinet in the new cabinet. Both he and the president were keen to bring in their own people. This, however, would have rendered me ineffective as prime minister. I could not chair a cabinet replete with people whose loyalty lay elsewhere.

Although the president was too accommodating of the speaker and was so perhaps in accordance with the Kampala Accord, I knew I needed his consent. He would not approve the cabinet I had selected unless Shariff Hassan was accommodated, and that created a serious challenge for me. The president and I had intense and sometimes heated discussions about the issue. He made it clear that the speaker should be accommodated, and I told him that this was not the right thing to do. I said, "I need to keep the majority of the cabinet I have appointed, and that will make it very difficult to bring some of the speaker's people on board." The president responded, "We have to find some room, and he will be part of the process, period." I was disappointed with his giving this extraordinary and unconstitutional role to the speaker. Nevertheless, the speaker had the tenacity to derail the process if he were not given a role in the formation of the cabinet. I reluctantly accepted this flawed arrangement.

Nevertheless the president and the speaker devised a way of dealing with me that I found disingenuous and deceitful. The president would call me and ask for a meeting, for example, around 8 p.m. But he would earlier have called the speaker to meet him at 6 p.m. Having finished their discussions by the time I arrived, the two men would have already decided how matters should progress.

Whenever I discovered that they had had a prior discussion, I challenged them and expressed my displeasure with their scheming. I would then leave, disgusted and dismayed. The duo would stay behind, discuss and deliberate what had transpired, and then commence conniving for the next day. That was the routine: they would meet before me, discuss, I would join, we would disagree, I would leave, and then they would stay behind, discuss further and come up with a new strategy of dealing with me the next day. It was extremely frustrating.

My biggest problem with this approach was that the president and speaker were trying to negate my high-caliber appointments to the cabinet and substitute them with people who I considered mediocre or who had a record of non-performance. I had a month to come up with a cabinet—a month in which to fight for my colleagues and push back the daily intrigues of these two gentlemen. They were conspiring to frustrate me until the thirty days expired, at which time the president would have the opportunity to nominate someone else who would be more amenable and more acquiescent to him. It was a tough and frustrating negotiation, and I had many sleepless nights as a result. Most of the people the president and speaker wanted to include in the cabinet had been members of the cabinet of Omar Abdirashid, Prime Minister Farmajo's predecessor.

Finally I realized that I had to compromise. The compromise was that neither the cabinet of Abdirashid nor the cabinet of Farmajo would be in the new government. This was completely unfair, because it would exclude people whom I knew to be almost one hundred well qualified for a role in the cabinet. I felt it was unjust and unwarranted to say that a hundred Somalis who had the right and the experience required to serve their country could not do so. There was no cause to exclude them from consideration. Unfortunately, the other option was that the president and the speaker would have the opportunity to choose their own man—a more amenable prime minister—as a result of my resignation or of the thirty-day period running out.

We all agreed that members of neither previous cabinet would return in the new cabinet. However, eliminating my choices and replacing them with mediocre people who had no track record was unacceptable to me, so I had to start from scratch. I called my friends and told them, "It is a difficult pill to swallow, it is unfair, and it doesn't serve the country or the interests of continuity for all the great work you have been doing. But a compromise has to be made. Otherwise, I will not be able to serve and neither will you. Since you're not returning to the cabinet, please give me your recommendations for the right person to replace you." Since the new cabinet would be based mainly on the 4.5 formula—a power-sharing arrangement whereby the four major clans in Somalia and the minority clans would share power—I asked them to pick representatives from their own clans. This was my strategy: to give my friends a stake in the new cabinet by giving them a say in choosing their replacements. It was the least I could do for them.

Fortunately, these "rejected" nominees showed themselves to

be statesmen. They readily proposed highly qualified replacements for themselves; in fact, one of them proposed three members of the eighteen-member cabinet. I was further relieved when the speaker and the president did not see a threat in the new selection and accepted my submissions. I never told them that I had asked my friends for recommendations, and I gave them a great deal of leeway in coming up with names that I would consider for the less important portfolios of deputy ministers and state ministers.

I accepted some of their suggestions and refused others, and finally a new cabinet was formed. I submitted the proposal to the president for his approval on July 19, and with his endorsement sent it to Parliament for approval on July 21, one day before the expiration of the 30-day window. I was glad that Shariff Hassan now felt that his wishes had been accommodated. He had a great deal of influence in Parliament, and we needed his support. Armed with our list of nominees, he worked hard for Parliament's approval and, fortunately, received it. I also submitted my political program for the country, a program that would later become the foundation for the Roadmap.

The new cabinet needed some time to become accustomed to Mogadishu. Most of its members were from the diaspora, and it was not easy for them to integrate quickly into an environment where there was no reliable security. Fortunately, most of the assistant ministers and state ministers were local, and they knew the terrain very well. They supported their ministers in ensuring that the essential work was done. However, we also had to find accommodation and transportation for them, and the government didn't have sufficient resources to cover their basic needs. It had other crises to deal with: the continuing war against al-Shabaab, and a devastating drought and subsequent famine.

Combating Al-Shabaab and Famine

Under the new administration, members of the military forces were receiving their salaries consistently and their morale improved. They were transformed from a ragtag militia into a fighting force willing to die for their country.

The security situation in Somalia improved as a result, and a sustained military drive was undertaken against al-Shabaab by the Somali National Army and AMISOM. The government believed that we first needed to defeat al-Shabaab militarily, and after that to fight it ideologically. By August 6, 2011, al-Shabaab had been forced to retreat from Mogadishu. Once Mogadishu was liberated, the government knew that al-Shabaab would not be able to maintain its strongholds outside the capital either. It was only a matter of time before al-Shabaab was defeated in other major urban centers: within a few months, it lost Baidoa, Beledwein, Afgoye, Balad, Merka, Hudur, Kismayo, Afmadow, and many more towns. It would take a while to completely eliminate al-Shabaab, but the trend was set.

However, the biggest challenge facing the TFG was a dry season that turned out to be the worst drought Somalia had experienced in sixty years. Because of the high level of desertification of an already semi-arid land, the drought had become cyclical and recurred every two years or so. At first, no one was aware of the drought's magnitude: Somalis didn't know its scale or how many lives it would affect. Eventually it became all too clear: the scale of the drought was in fact overwhelming, and it soon resulted in a widespread famine that affected more than half of Somalia's population, particularly in the six states south of Mogadishu. As the crops failed, starving people streamed into the capital city in the thousands. Many of them perished on the way; some families lost almost all their children. Families that once had seven children now only had one or two left.

It was a gut-wrenching experience, harrowing and disturbing. My unique position as prime minister allowed me to see things that others might not be in a position to see, and it affected me deeply. Mogadishu itself wasn't severely affected by the drought, but the internally displaced from the countryside, having no food and no shelter, were scattered all over the city. I had never seen suffering of that magnitude. Furthermore, the displaced were defecating on the streets and in public parks, a practice that threatened to spread communicable diseases and became a health hazard for the entire city.

I summoned the UN agencies and international NGOs in Mogadishu and briefed them about the magnitude of this catastrophe. The UN personnel appeared to be oblivious to the plight of those affected by the drought. They were protected in their sheltered environments and seemed to have no idea of what was going on in the countryside. They were receiving second-hand reports but did not directly witnessing the magnitude of the tragedy unfolding outside their gates. They either didn't know or didn't care; I cannot say for certain.

When I informed them of the seriousness of the famine, they said: "We will make an assessment, evaluate the situation, and send a report to Nairobi. Then Nairobi will relay the information to New York." I thought this response was reckless and irresponsible; we were experiencing an emergency. Their assessment of "the situation" and correspondence with Nairobi and New York could take months; meanwhile, people were dying in the thousands. Most of the UN staff in Mogadishu were junior officials, not the decision makers, who were in Nairobi and in New York. These distant decision makers were not willing to visit Mogadishu to see the problem on the ground and get firsthand information. They had no desire to come to Mogadishu and thus relied on information provided by their junior staff in Mogadishu. There was too much bureaucracy; the modus operandi of the UN was not suited to the task. People needed food, shelter, and clothing. In short, they needed immediate relief and quickly.

Those few agencies with emergency relief available had rations sufficient to feed a few thousand people, but not tens of thousands. This relief could last for only a few days. I summoned the UN agencies and international NGOs personnel to my office again and again, and repeatedly told them about the crisis we were facing. They shrugged their shoulders, unmoved by the tragic loss of so many Somali lives.

I finally came to the conclusion that we would have to rely on ourselves and use our own meager resources. We had a meeting of the cabinet, the president, the speaker, and myself, and decided that all available resources—even our own salaries—would be allocated to the relief effort. Unfortunately, the timing couldn't have been worse. The whole government revenue came from only two sources, Mogadishu's port and airport. The period between June and September is the worst time in terms of government revenue: it is the monsoon season, when powerful winds deter commercial boats and dhows from docking in the port of Mogadishu. Only the big ships that can weather the storms enter the port and dock there. Thus government revenue declined by more than 80 percent between June and September 2011.

It was a "perfect storm": a disaster was unfolding in the droughts and the resulting malnutrition and starvation; the UN agencies and international and local NGOs were either not able or not willing to help; and government revenue declined precipitously. There was perhaps less than $100,000 in Somalia's treasury. So we decided to allocate the first available $500,000 for immediate relief. We were expecting the revenue for the next few weeks to be approximately that amount, so clearly all of it would have to be allotted to the relief effort. We projected that this amount would sustain the displaced in Mogadishu for a couple of weeks, while we waited for a response from our appeal to the international community—an appeal that the president and I made the next day.

With the initial $500,000, we established the first two relief camps, collected people from the city, and brought them to the camps. The first camp, Badbaado, or "Salvation," housed around 30,000 people, and the second, Rajo, or "Hope," held 15,000–20,000 people. We were able to secure the camps and provide tents, food, and water for their inhabitants. Although the health hazard continued, the death toll declined when we started providing relief.

Within three weeks of our appeal, the images of the death and despair in Somalia had reached everywhere internationally, and our joint appeal to the international community brought a swift and positive response. International dignitaries started to come to Mogadishu. The first to arrive in support was the president of Djibouti, Ismail Omar Guelleh. He was followed by the prime minister of Turkey, Recep Tayyip Erdogan, who arrived while al-Shabaab still occupied some parts of Mogadishu, such as Daynile and the outlying districts of the city. Entering Mogadishu at this time was daring. Nevertheless Erdogan came with his wife, his children, and a large delegation. It was an enormous security challenge because we never knew where al-Shabaab was; its members could be anywhere. But Erdogan was a kind and compassionate man. He would, for example, sometimes ask a convoy to stop so that he could step out of his vehicle and speak to an emaciated old woman sitting on the sidewalk.

Other dignitaries arrived as well, including the foreign minister of Iran. The relief efforts continued to produce results, but now another huge challenge arose: the diversion of the relief by a coalition of gangs, district commissioners, police, and the military. Everyone wanted to put their hands on the relief—it was free food— and everyone was keen on having a share of the bounty. How could we deal with this criminal enterprise mushrooming around the relief effort? Some of the nastier gangs in the city would collect people as token refugees, establish a small camp, and appoint themselves as the gatekeepers. Then they would ask for a cut of the relief from the people in the camps. Perhaps 30 to 40 percent of the food relief was diverted by these gatekeepers. It did not simplify matters that they, the district commissioners, and the district police were working hand in glove with each other.

The situation in Mogadishu did, however, become stabilized, and about 80 percent of the city was now under government control. The problem remained in the countryside, south of Mogadishu, and in some areas north of the city. Al-Shabaab controlled all of south-central Somalia, from Dhobley on the Kenyan border to Mogadishu, except for a few districts in Gedo. It refused to let the relief food get through to reach those who needed it most. That made the situation much worse. Even those refugees who could walk might perish on the road. Finally, al-Shabaab realized that it was not politically convenient to deny the relief to the drought-affected populations under its control. Al-Shabaab members themselves were affected by the drought and reluctantly decided to allow some relief to reach the intended recipients. Fortunately we found some local NGOs willing to deliver relief to those areas.

We spoke to the countries neighboring Somalia about their willingness to provide assistance in getting relief to affected areas, and they were very helpful. For example, we couldn't get relief from Mogadishu to Gedo because al-Shabaab controlled a large swath of land between the two areas. I asked Kenya's prime minister, Raila Odinga, for permission to land relief aircraft in Wajir and then to transport the food from there to southern Somalia. He immediately agreed.

As a result of Somalia's security efforts, al-Shabaab was licking its wounds. The sustained campaign by AMISOM and the Somali army was paying off. The war effort didn't slow at any moment; the troops continued pounding al-Shabaab so that it would be kept at bay during this time of national emergency. It put up a real resistance in Daynile, where in one day its members killed more than seventy Burundian military personnel, but eventually al-Shabaab was defeated there as well.

The affairs of state continued, but the relief effort occupied a great deal of time that could have been devoted to political programs. When the drought situation stabilized in September, it was time to tend to the other responsibilities of state. We had a lot of work to do because we had an extensive political program. Besides dealing with the famine, fighting al-Shabaab, and ensuring that Somalia was liberated and stabilized, we needed to bring Somalis together for a united purpose and to keep the government together by developing smooth working relationships among the speaker, the president, and Parliament.

The key challenges here included the fact that the time I had available to act was extremely short. I had only a year, I was armed with very limited resources, and the task was immense. We needed to finalize the constitution, undertake a continuing relief effort for the drought-affected population, continue to improve the security situation of the country, provide leadership and political reconciliation among Somalis, and establish good governance institutions. It was a daunting prospect, complicated by the reality of clan politics.

BRINGING THE STAKEHOLDERS TOGETHER:

ESTABLISHING THE PROTOCOLS

Gathering the Principals in Mogadishu

One of the most pressing issues for the government in 2011was to bring the main Somali stakeholders to the same table so that they could discuss the decisions the country had to make in order to move it forward. The challenge here was that most of the principals could not agree on how to accomplish this.

The Kampala Accord had brought the speaker of the Parliament, Shariff Hassan Sheikh Aden, and the president, Sheikh Sharif Sheikh Ahmed closer. The next step was to bring other principal stakeholders on board. Somaliland had made it clear that it wanted nothing to do with the rest of Somalia. Its leaders weren't interested in the conversation we wanted to have, and therefore we could not involve them. We decided to leave them to pursue their separatist agenda and instead started with the two states that had some modicum of administration: Puntland and Galmudug.

The president of Puntland, Abdirahman Mohamed Farole, had difficulty in developing a relationship with TFG president Sheikh Sharif. Farole believed that he controlled a peaceful area comprising roughly one third of Somali territory, whereas Sheikh Sharif was the "president of Mogadishu"—in fact, not even all of Mogadishu in this view. Farole felt that Sheikh Sharif controlled neither a territory nor a population. In short, Farole believed that he was more legitimate and thus more important than Sheikh Sharif.

On the other hand, Sheikh Sharif believed that he was the president of an internationally recognized government—that he was the president of all Somalia, including Puntland. He thought that Farole was simply the governor of a small part of Somalia, and he felt a deep resentment about Farole's lack of respect for him. I thought that Farole was suffering from a superiority complex while Sheikh Sharif was equally suffering from an inferiority complex, and I decided to handle the situation accordingly.

It was incumbent upon on me, as someone hailing from Puntland, to at least bring Puntland and the TFG closer. It was a delicate issue that needed to be handled with care and a well-crafted mediation strategy. Generally, I would go to Sheikh Sharif and ask him to pick up the telephone and call Farole. Sheikh Sharif was eager to improve his relationship with Farole. He would readily pick up the phone, and they would speak for an hour or so. Sheikh Sharif was a good listener and Farole was a good talker—it was a match made in heaven.

The next day I would call Farole and tell him he needed to be more respectful of the president and show some deference to the head of state. Disrespecting Sheikh Sharif would not serve any purpose, except to create more animosity and aggravate the situation. Now I would ask him to pick up the telephone and call Sheikh Sharif. Then I would go to the president and tell him, "Farole will call you. I want you to please pick up the phone when he calls and talk to him."

I continued to play this mediation role, first talking to one and then to the other. Slowly the two leaders began to warm to each other, and after a couple of months of my back-and-forth intercessions they were comfortable with one another. At that point, the end of August 2011, I decided to take Sheikh Sharif along on a visit to Puntland. This would be his first time visit to any part of Somalia other than Mogadishu.

I traveled to Garowe three days ahead of Sheikh Sharif's arrival to pave the way for him and convinced Farole and the government of Puntland to give him the reception he deserved. Sheikh Sharif didn't know what to expect from Puntland or, for that matter, from Farole, so he intended to simply come and go in one day, and not to spend the night.

When he arrived in Garowe, Sheikh Sharif couldn't believe what he saw: the people of the city were lined up on the sides of the streets to greet him. They were clapping and chanting, and his pictures were visible all over Garowe. Sheikh Sharif was so warmly received that he was overtaken by emotion. He got out of his car, walked among the crowds, and greeted people. We walked at least two kilometers. I think that, after the experience of being in lockdown in Mogadishu, he was relieved to come to this peaceful part of the country where people received him warmly. This trip demonstrated to him that his influence wasn't limited to the few square kilometers of Mogadishu and that another part of the country also regarded him as the nation's president.

However, because of the security protocols put in place by AMISOM, he could not after all stay overnight in Puntland. The protocols required advance notice for an overnight stay so that the relevant security measures could be put in place. Since Sheikh Sharif had told everyone he wouldn't be spending the night, AMISOM had prepared accordingly. When Farole found out that Sheikh Sharif wouldn't be staying overnight, even after being so well received in Garowe, he reacted as if he had been slapped in the face. He could not understand why Sheikh Sharif wouldn't stay.

With the help of some of his close associates, I convinced Farole that Sheikh Sharif couldn't spend the night—not because he didn't want to, but because of the security arrangements put in place by AMISOM. I implied that it was AMISOM's mistake and not Sheikh Sharif's fault, because I could not envision going back to square one with these men. Fortunately, Farole accepted this and the president returned to Mogadishu without incident.

I stayed in Garowe for an additional day before traveling to Galkayo to meet with President Caalin of Galmudug. I wanted to bring Caalin on board as well because he too had a rocky relationship with Sheikh Sharif, feeling that Sheikh Sharif did not respect him enough. Farole and Caalin had made an agreement in Garowe six months earlier, on February 18, to question the legitimacy of the TFG and to undermine Sheikh Sharif's authority as the president of the country. Both men had a very territorial mindset: I control this area/I control that area; I am the president of Galmudug/I am the president of Puntland; therefore I have to be respected accordingly. It was a real challenge—the center versus the periphery.

I wanted to ensure that these men too were getting along, in order to prepare the groundwork for the meeting in Mogadishu that would bring all the Somali stakeholders together to develop the Roadmap. So I invited Caalin to Mogadishu. He gracefully accepted, "even though I am having difficulties with your president," he explained. Caalin was very humble and easy to get along with, so I replied, "Let us set aside these personal differences and work for the common good."

I also had to convince Ahlu Sunna Wal Jama'aa (ASWJ), a moderate religious group that was also fighting al-Shabaab in central Somalia and Gedo, to participate. The members of ASWJ practice a more traditional, Sufi-style Islam and were against al-Shabaab's austere version of Islam. Al-Shabaab had waged war on the Sufis and desecrated the tombs of Sufi religious scholars. ASWJ as a result declared war on al-Shabaab and its encroachment in central and southwestern Somalia. Its members put up a very stiff resistance, and to some extent supported the TFG forces in Mogadishu.

Fortunately, everyone we invited to Mogadishu accepted, and we met there from September 4 to 6, 2011. Caalin and Farole arrived on the same day. Farole came on the condition that he would not be under the protection of the TFG but rather under the protection of AMISOM. I told him he would be staying at Villa Somalia, which fell under AMISOM protection. Sheikh Sharif had been gracious enough to move one of his families from one of the villas so that Farole and Caalin could stay there.

However, Farole appeared to want to "repay" Sheikh Sharif for not having stayed in Garowe earlier. He said he would attend the opening ceremony for the Roadmap but would fly back to Garowe the same day. He would not spend the night. I said to him, "Mr. President, you are more mature than that. You came here to patch up a broken country and not to make a point. That is immature and unbecoming of a president." Eventually, after some discussion, Farole was convinced to stay overnight at Villa Somalia and to leave the next day.

Using the Roadmap to Move Beyond Transition

The Roadmap was a detailed list of dozens of tasks designed to steer Somalia out of the transition period and toward more permanent political institutions and greater national security and stability. It included various measures in many areas: countering piracy, co-opting local militia groups, preventing the recruitment of children into armed groups, demarcating the territorial waters of Somalia, reducing the size of Parliament, developing peace-building initiatives, and tackling corruption. Announced in Mogadishu on September 6, 2011, the Roadmap was initialed by me, the leaders of Puntland and Galmudug, the head of the ASWJ militia group, the UN envoy to Somalia, representatives of the League of Arab States, the African Union (AU) and the Inter-Governmental Authority on Development (IGAD).

Somalia had been trapped in a dreadful period of instability for almost thirteen years because there was no political framework to guide the country out of this state of affairs. I never understood why the nation had been put in this terrible situation in the first place.

Other countries known as "fragile states," such as Liberia, Sierra Leone, and Burundi, were in a similar situation, yet they maintained permanent status for their governments throughout their turmoil. What was so peculiar about Somalia that it should be subjected to this demeaning status? No one could tell me. The whole transitional arrangement was shrouded in mystery.

Nevertheless certain requirements needed to be fulfilled to complete a framework that would guide Somalia out of the transition. First, commitment; there must be a government with a leadership committed to ending the transition. Second, a framework must be put in place, with deadlines and benchmarks; otherwise the days would pass without progress. Somalia had never made a serious commitment to end the transition, and as a result there was no framework to do so.

As stakeholders, we all wanted to move beyond the transition, but we had to come up with a mechanism. We had no literature to work with. We needed to set benchmarks and deadlines in order to complete tasks on time. To do so, we assigned responsibility, resources, and compliance mechanisms in the Roadmap, the first undertaking to emerge from transition. The Roadmap was composed of four key areas, the same areas outlined in the political program I submitted to Parliament at the time of my confirmation:

- Security
- Draft Constitution for Adoption by a National Constituent Assembly
- Political Outreach and Reconciliation
- Good Governance and Institutions

Each of these areas is discussed in detail below.

Security

Security was our number one priority. The government could not focus on any of its objectives if the security was not there. It needed a breathing space so that it could function. This involved securing Somalia from al-Shabaab and having an effective maritime and counter-piracy policy and strategy.

Without security, the rest of the Roadmap could not be achieved: elections would not be held, the constitution would not be ratified or adopted, and there would be no way to establish good governance institutions. The key tasks we identified as part of the security benchmark included the following:

- An inclusive Joint Security Committee (JSC) that would hold bi-monthly meetings in Mogadishu to address the key security issues and challenges facing Somalia.
- A National Security and Stabilization Plan (NSSP) to be approved and implemented by October 19, 2011.
- Effective maritime security and counter-piracy policy and legislation to be drawn up in conjunction with regional entities, including Puntland and Somaliland, and to be established by January 20, 2012, to prevent piracy and protect Somalia's natural resources.

Realizing that al-Shabaab was a highly mobile force that moved from place to place—for instance, fighting in Hudur one day and in Burhakaba the next—we developed a strategy whereby we would both push in on the enemy from the center and the periphery. Its forces would be put in a squeeze and thus would not have the luxury of moving around. Since we had forces in Jubba, Gedo, Bay, and Bakol, as well as in central Somalia (particularly the ASWJ forces there), we began to push al-Shabaab from Mogadishu and pull its forces from the periphery, particularly in the southern and central regions, in order to trap them.

This strategy was already being implemented in and around Mogadishu. A few months earlier, in June 2011, al-Shabaab had been less than a kilometer from Villa Somalia and the government had controlled less than 50 percent of the capital. By August 6, al-Shabaab had vacated most of Mogadishu and was on the run— its forces lost more and more territory and finally had to resort to guerrilla tactics. We believed that if this strategy were continued it would produce a remarkable series of events, and so it did. During the next several months, we were able to expel al-Shabaab from all the important urban centers, liberating Mogadishu, Bal'ad, Afgoye, Baidoa, Hudur, Beletweyne, Kismayo, Afmadow, and the whole Gedo region except for several towns.

Draft Constitution for Adoption by a National Constituent Assembly

Although an approved Somali constitution did not yet exist, a draft had been under way with the Independent Federal Constitution Commission (IFCC) for almost six years. So far, it had cost $50 million. It had become a project for 'experts' based in Nairobi, particularly some UN agencies and international NGOs, and their collaborators in Somalia. There was no real commitment to finalize it and submit it for adoption. To end the transition and for the new political dispensation to occur in August 2012, we needed to draft a constitution and submit it to a "constituent assembly" for final adoption.

On September 19, 2011, I appointed a committee of experts, based mainly on the 4.5 clan formula but including Somali lawyers, political scientists, economists, and Islamic scholars, to speed up the process. They would take over from the IFCC. Since large swathes of Somalia were still controlled by al-Shabaab at that time, security remained a problem, and we decided that the constitution should be adopted not by referendum but by proxy. A National Constituent Assembly (NCA) would do this instead. The NCA would consist of 825 Somalis, from all walks of life and from all over the country, and encompass all the important focus groups, such as religious leaders, traditional leaders, the business community, women's groups, youth, the diaspora, NGOs—particularly local NGOs—and local administrations.

The 825 NCA members were to be selected not by the government but by the country's traditional leaders. We felt that traditional leaders, the moral authority of the country, would be the only people popularly perceived as objective enough to select the NCA members without prejudice. Although some traditional leaders were considered biased, particularly those hailing from the secessionist entity of Somaliland, they were the best people we could get under the circumstances. We hoped our reliance on them, instead of on political leaders, would avoid any perception of conflicts of interest.

The Roadmap stipulated that a draft constitution had to be submitted to the constituent assembly by April 20, 2012. I asked the committee of experts to prepare a first draft by February 20 so that the final draft would be ready by April. I urged them to respect the deadline so that progress would not be slowed, as had occurred before, and —lo and behold—we had a final draft constitution ready by April 20.

Bringing the 825 NCA members to Mogadishu to adopt the constitution in July was a logistical nightmare. We had no budget and it was a low season in terms of government revenue, so we were counting on assistance from our traditional partners. But we did not get the support we needed from the international community— although they had promised assistance to cover the costs of accommodation, food, and per diems for the 825 members of the NCA. Once we realized that we were on our own, we pulled up our sandal straps and sought loans and credit from Somali businessmen. They delivered their promised assistance to us. Sadly, however, some of these good men have not yet been repaid.

Nevertheless, by August 1 the constitution was enthusiastically adopted, with a 96 percent vote of support from the NCA members. It was still a provisional constitution—and it will not be a real constitution until a referendum will have been held throughout Somalia —but now we had what we needed: a provisional constitution as a basis for the elections and the new political dispensation scheduled for later that month.

One of the issues addressed in the constitution was the reform of Parliament. Parliament is the mother of all the constitutional branches of the country; in Somalia it is Parliament that elects the president, and it is the president who nominates the prime minister. In the past we had had a Parliament that was not deserving of Somalia; it included warlords, criminals, and members who were functionally illiterate. The Roadmap signatories appointed a twenty-seven-member Technical Selection Committee (TSC) to decide who would sit in the 275 member Parliament. As the gatekeeper, the TSC decided that members of Parliament should fulfill the criteria stipulated in the Garowe principles (see chapter 6, "Implementing the Roadmap"). The elders tasked to select the new members of Parliament were not well versed in these criteria and were susceptible to the manipulation of those seeking seats. The TSC was given the authority to review the candidates and to support the elders in selecting individuals who met the criteria.

The criteria stipulated that the members of Parliament must have no history of criminality or warlordism, a minimum level of education, such as a high school diploma or equivalent experience, and a good moral compass. We did not want known drug barons, for example, to be sitting in Parliament.

However, a problem arose. The Roadmap signatories did not all agree on these criteria. I adamantly opposed all efforts that would enable the warlords and those excluded by the TSC to take seats in the new Parliament, whereas the president, Sheikh Sharif, fought tooth and nail to bring his warlord supporters on board. He was desperately seeking votes for his re-election, and by any means necessary. The TSC, it must be said, also made mistakes and judged some fully qualified individuals as warlords and misfits. Thus, I was caught in the middle—between the TSC, which was applying very stringent criteria yet making some errors, and the president, who was desperately seeking votes.

Ultimately, all those excluded by the TSC made it into Parliament. Because of the political tussle between the president and myself, a compromise was reached to nominate a parliamentary committee that would look into the issue of disqualification and address the dispute over selection criteria. However, to the dismay of the TSC and everyone else working for a better Parliament, the newly elected speaker of the house Mohamed Jawari and the president, at the last minute before the presidential election, let all those disqualified by the TSC into Parliament. Thus, warlords and other unqualified candidates were ultimately permitted to be sworn in as members of Parliament only an hour before the election of the president was about to commence.

I believe the new speaker of Parliament was "repaying" me for our disagreements on the draft constitution. At the time I was unaware that he resented my desire to speed up the process and conclude the transition. I can safely say that Sheikh Shariff won on this subterfuge and increased his chances of winning the election by twenty votes. Ultimately, Parliament was downsized from 550 to 275 members. However, reduction doesn't necessarily mean reform, and that was the case with the latter Somali Parliament.

Political Outreach and Reconciliation

Somalia remained fragmented into clan-based fiefdoms, and without reconciliation there was no way the country could move forward. The most defining feature of this reconciliation benchmark was getting people together. To do this, we needed a concerted effort: the center (the TFG) and the periphery (regional administrations) must work together. There were known regional administrations, such as Puntland and Galmudug, but there were also other emerging states, and they had to work in unison and in harmony. Key tasks in this area included the following:

- The TFG, in consultation with regional entities including the ASWJ, was to prepare a national reconciliation plan for resolving inter-clan disputes and for proposing an inclusive outreach strategy to be approved by Parliament by October 1, 2011.

- The National Reconciliation Commission was to be reformed and revitalized by October 1, 2011.

- Support was to be provided to regional entities, including the ASWJ, to establish and coordinate local-level reconciliation and peace-building initiatives across the country by November 19, 2011.

- Subject to security, all regions under the TFG and allied regional entities were to be visited by the government by November 19, 2011, and/or modalities for establishing and supporting local administrations were to be set up.

- Pre-existing peace committees were to be reactivated within regional entities, and new ones were to be established by November 19, 2011, to facilitate local/grass roots reconciliation and peace-building initiatives.

As previously mentioned, one of the priorities of my government was to stabilize newly liberated areas. To do so, we needed to establish "peace committees" in those areas to start reconciling the community. We could then proceed to establish some modicum of local administration, which would eventually lead to the formation of regional administrations. We could then in turn deliver humanitarian and social services, including health services, education, water, and sanitation to needy people. It was imperative that the TFG should be a better alternative than al-Shabaab for doing this.

Good Governance and Institutions

It is said that politics and state building are all about institutions. Good institutions beget good governance, and good governance is the essence of statehood, nationhood, and development. Good governance institutions should reflect transparency and accountability, fight corruption and malfeasance, and establish public finance management systems so that the resources of the country will be managed wisely.

Somalia was in a state of disarray because of the collapse of all state institutions. The government had absolutely nothing to work with; there were ministers but no bureaucracy, and no regulatory entities, so we were starting from zero. Those who had gotten rid of Siad Barre in Mogadishu, the USC particularly, were not interested in institution building and had destroyed all the institutions of government. They perceived the government as an occupier of their rightful space and thought of all ministries and government institutions as creations of Siad Barre, and thus undesirable. It was severely shortsighted on their part.

To counter this misapprehension, key tasks in this benchmark of the Roadmap included:

- Enhancing mechanisms for greater coordination and information sharing between Somali and international development and humanitarian agencies by September 19, 2011.

- Enacting legislation and implementing measures to fight corruption and the abuse of public offices at all levels of government, including local and regional governments by October 19, 2011.

- Appointing competent members of an interim Independent Anti-Corruption Commission (maximum of nine members, including four women) by November 19, 2011.

- Appointing a competent task force by December 19, 2011, to prepare a report of all TFG revenues, receipts, and expenditures, airport taxes, landing fees, parking fees, over-flight fees, port fees and charges, including wharfage charges and fees, telecommunications, and revenues from donors.

- Ensuring that all government revenues were collected through the use of official government documents, were recorded according to the law, and were deposited to the Consolidated Fund at the Central Bank by December 19, 2011.

- Completing a comprehensive report on all TFG revenues and expenditures to be completed by January 20, 2012.

- Reviewing and updating the existing Civil Service Code/Law by January 20, 2012.

- Formulating and approving a National Fiscal Budget for the year 2011/2012 by December 31, 2011.

- Initiating the process to develop a National Development and Recovery Strategy by February 20, 2012.

I appointed an Anti-Corruption Committee of nine people (four women and five men) on January 19, 2012. In March, the president approved the appointment and issued a presidential decree legalizing this committee and giving it full investigative powers. In the meantime, I proposed a Financial Integrity Board or Mutual Accountability Board to build confidence with our traditional donors. A billion dollars had been spent in the name of Somalia annually, with no substantive change occurring on the ground through the efforts of either the UN agencies or international NGOs.

Someone has described the behavior of the "Nairobi mafia" of aid agencies to be like that of a possessive foster family. In the West, the child of dysfunctional parents might be taken away by social services and given to a foster family, which is provided with money to take care of the child. However, when the parents are no longer dysfunctional, the foster family may want to keep the child because it is making money from the situation. It might not allow the parents to resume the upbringing of their own child. Similarly, the Somali government is labeled dysfunctional and the purse strings are held by Nairobi. Even if Somalis are willing to put their house in order, the Nairobi mafia will not relinquish control of the situation.

I proposed a Mutual Accountability Board so that Somalia could be accountable to the international community and its donors with regard to where the money was spent. The locally generated revenue was not a great deal of money—$2 million per month at the most, or less than $24 million a year. But where does the $1 billion in humanitarian relief and development aid go every year? As Mark Bowden, the United Nations humanitarian coordinator for Somalia told me, the UN spent an average of $250 million a

Second (II) ISTANBUL CONFERENCE ON SOMALIA, Turkish Prime Minister Recep Tayyip Erdogan meeting with Somali Prime Minister Abdiweli Mohamed Ali May 31, 2012 Istanbul, Turkey

Left to right UN Special Representative for Somalia Mahiga, Somali Parliament Speaker Aden, Somali President Ahmed, Somali PM Ali, Puntland President Farole in Nairobi, Kenya, June 22, 2012. Agreement on the Draft Federal Republic of Somalia Provisional Constitution

Second (II) Istanbul Conference on Somalia Turkish Prime Minister Recep Tayyip Erdogan meeting with Somali Prime Minister Abdiweli Mohamed Ali, May 31, 2012, Istanbul, Turkey

year on development in the six years from 2005 to 2011. But on the development of what? Not a single school was built, not a single hospital was built, and not one kilometer of road was paved. Where did the money go?

Although I had asked our international partners for a mutual accountability board (what later became the Joint Financial Management Board, or JFMB), they were interested only in unilateral accountability. The British ambassador, Matt Baugh, was particularly obsessed with the JFMB. Basically, western donors to Somalia wanted to know where and how our meager resources were being spent, but no questions were to be asked about the $1 billion spent in the name of Somalia every year. This paternalistic view of the western donors was condescending and patronizing, bordering on modern-day colonization.

I felt the JFMB was being disingenuous and hypocritical and that Somalis could not let others dictate to us where the few million dollars was to be spent. Nevertheless the donors were fixated on the JFMB and took it to every forum and platform they could, including the London Conference of February 2012. Ultimately they convinced the UN Security Council to unilaterally impose this one-sided hegemonic agenda on Somalia.

IMPLEMENTING THE ROADMAP:

MEETINGS ALONG THE WAY

Conferring with Outsiders and Insiders

After the Roadmap was agreed on September 2011, the government of Somalia needed to start implementing it. That would be a long road, involving consultations with various groups both locally and internationally. Along the way, the following meetings I attended and addressed—most of them positive and consensus-building gatherings and conferences—are of note.

- Addressing the UN Security Council in New York (September 2011)
- Meeting with the Somali Diaspora in Washington, Virginia, and Toronto (September 2011)
- Addressing the UN General Assembly in New York (September 2011)
- Attending the International Contact Group Meeting in Copenhagen (September 2011)
- Attending the Garowe 1 Conference (December 2011)
- Attending the Garowe 2 Conference (February 2012)
- Attending the London Conference (February 2012)
- Attending the Istanbul Conference (May 2012)
- Attending the Addis Ababa and Nairobi Principals' Meetings (May–June 2012)

These events are discussed in detail in the following pages.

Visiting the United Nations Security Council

An appearance at the United Nations was the TFG's opportunity to announce to the world our agreement on the Roadmap and our firm intention to bring the transition to a successful completion by August 2012. I left Mogadishu in the second week of September 2011 to brief the UN Security Council on the situation in Somalia. We had just concluded the Roadmap conference in Mogadishu on September 6, only one month after securing the city from Al-Shabaab.

It was my first visit to the UN as a prime minister. I wanted to ensure that our new policy, direction, and new Roadmap would be understood by the international community and would garner their support. The Roadmap entailed a commitment from us, but we also needed a commitment from the international community in terms of financial contributions and political support. I was also looking for a buy-in from the Security Council with regard to our new agenda for the country.

The UN special representative to Somalia, Augustine Mahiga, was in New York as well to provide input. Mahiga was a former Tanzanian permanent representative at the UN. He was committed both to the Roadmap and to Somalia's overall success. A very good listener, he had played a role as mediator in Somalia's irksome and elusive reconciliation efforts. Moreover, he was a good friend of President Yoweri Museveni of Uganda, the country that had the largest contingent of AMISOM forces in Somalia and thus was the largest international stakeholder in both the Roadmap and the peace process in Somalia.

At this time, the UN Security Council didn't know what to expect from the new government of Somalia. The last time we had appeared there, in March 2011, I had accompanied the former prime minister, Mohamed Abdullahi Farmajo, and we had not receive a good reception. Somalis were too fragmented politically then. We were accused of being not inclusive enough and not accommodating enough to other Somali stakeholders.

On this occasion, the Security Council was aware that the president and I had visited Garowe; that in Mogadishu the Roadmap had been signed by all the stakeholders; and that Farole, Caalin, and the ASWJ had all come to Mogadishu and witnessed the unveiling of the Roadmap. They knew there were much progress on the political front and some progress on the security front. Moreover, Mahiga was constantly briefing them. His knowledge and credibility made them aware of the big picture.

My aim was to garner support from the international community to mitigate the devastating effect of the drought and receive the necessary backing for the fight against al-Shabaab. I wanted to create a breathing space for the government to function; it was indispensable to capture more territory to increase the reach of the government, particularly in south-central Somalia. We were required to have elections in less than a year, so we needed a secure and stable environment to bring the political process to fruition.

The Security Council, after discussing and deliberating the Roadmap documents, readily endorsed the Roadmap. But to completing the Roadmap tasks needed more than approval; it required firm commitments and support from the international community. This is what I wanted to convey in my remarks to the Security Council on September 14, 2011 which were well received (see Appendix A). I also met UN Secretary General Ban Ki Moon to brief him about recent developments in Somalia. He was very committed to the peace and development of Somalia and made a pledge to visit the country, a pledge he fulfilled on December 9, 2011. This was one of the best meetings for promoting Somalia's future, as it addressed a number of issues, including the progress on the ground in terms of security, political outreach, reconciliation, and more importantly the Roadmap signed by all the key stakeholders.

Visiting the Somali Diaspora in Washington, Virginia, and Toronto

One day after my briefing of the Security Council, I left for Washington, D.C., to visit the U.S. Congress and meet with the Somali diaspora in the Washington metropolitan area. I met separately with three members of the U.S. Congress—Donald Payne, Chris Smith, and Keith Ellison—and briefed them on the situation in Somalia and recent successes in security, political outreach, reconciliation, the high-level meeting in Mogadishu, the drought, and the humanitarian situation, as well as the Roadmap. We discussed the best ways in which the U.S. government could support Somalia at this critical juncture in its history. All three Congressmen were very supportive and congratulated me for accepting what they called "the toughest job in the world." They agreed to write a letter to the U.S. State Department and the UN to push for the critical reinforcement of AMISOM and for the strengthening of the Somali armed forces.

I knew it was important to engage the Somali diaspora, to get their support and commitment. Not surprisingly, I found them to be very inquisitive about the situation in Somalia and sometimes very skeptical that anything good could be accomplished there at this time. I briefed them about the new direction we were taking, especially the Roadmap. I expressed our firm belief that Somalis in the diaspora were key stakeholders in Somalia; therefore, it was imperative that they and the government should work together to bring about peace and stability in the country.

On September 18, I traveled to Toronto to meet with the Somali community there. As was the case in Washington, most members of the diaspora here harbored suspicions about Somali governments, past and present. They wanted Somalia to succeed but had been disillusioned and disheartened by the previous political failures. In the Somali diaspora, cynicism abounds and it must be admitted that its members could not be blamed for attributing the ills of Somalia to the current crop of leaders.

Attending the UN General Assembly

On September 20, I returned to New York to attend the annual meeting of United Nations General Assembly. On the same day I met Kevin Rudd, then the foreign minister of Australia. Australia has made a substantial contribution to the relief effort in Somalia via the World Food Program. We discussed the situation in Somalia and the relations between the two countries. The minister had recently visited Dolow in southwestern Somalia and had seen the suffering of the drought-affected Somali refugees. Australia was standing for election in the Security Council for 2013 and 2014, and Rudd asked Somalia to support Australia in its candidacy.

The annual meeting of the UN General Assembly was officially opened on September 21. My delegation, including deputy prime minister and minister of foreign affairs, Mohamed Mohamoud Sheikh Ibrahim, and I participated in the whole session. I also met Italy's minister of foreign affairs, H.E. Franco Frattini, and discussed bilateral relations between Somalia and Italy. The minister indicated that Italy fully supported the TFG and that the international community needed to do more to help Somalia with development projects in the areas of agriculture, education, and health. We signed a historic agreement in which Italy donated about €15 million to Somalia as part of a previous agreement between the two countries. The minister stated that Italy would continue to support Somalia by paying the salaries of three thousand soldiers, supporting the capacity-building of the ministries, and helping Somalia to mobilize resources from the international community. He invited me to officially meet the prime minister of Italy, H.E. Mario Monti, in

Rome.

I also held bilateral talks with the president of Gabon, Ali Bongo; the prime minister of Turkey, Recep Tayyip Erdogan; the prime minister of Qatar, Hamid bin Jassim Al-thani; the under-secretary-general of the UN, Valerie Amos; the African Union peace and security commissioner, Ramtane Lammamra; the Organization of Islamic Conference secretary-general, Ekmeleddin Ihsanoglu; the minister of foreign affairs of Oman, Yusuf bin Alawi bin Abdullah; the under-secretary-general of the UN, Lynn Pascoe; as well as the UN secretary general, H.E. Ban Ki-Moon, whom I had met on my previous visit to New York, among others.

Prime Minister Erdogan reconfirmed Turkey's financial commitment to Somalia. He averred that the Turkish International Development Agency and the Turkish Red Crescent were already in Mogadishu and underscored that Turkey would soon open its embassy there. The prime minister indicated that Turkey wanted to be an example to others and that his deputy prime minister, Bekir Bozdag, would be in charge of the Somalia projects. Immediate work by the Turks would include rebuilding Mogadishu's airport, roads, hospitals, and schools. The prime minister reiterated that Bekir would visit Mogadishu every two months and report directly to him. Turkey would soon send significant number of heavy vehicles to Somalia, and already five garbage trucks were on their way.

On September 23, the UN secretary general chaired a summit on Somalia. This meeting included the participation of the presidents of Kenya and Burundi, the vice-president of Uganda, the chairperson of the African Union, the UN secretary general and under-secretary-general, U.S. Secretary of State Hillary Clinton, U.K. Foreign Secretary William Hague, the ministers of foreign affairs of Turkey, Djibouti, and Ethiopia, and the secretary general of the Arab League. Participants also included representatives of France, Germany, Spain, Sudan, Sweden, the European Union, and the Organization of Islamic Cooperation. They discussed the current situation of Somalia and the way forward.

On September 24, Ban Ki-Moon convened a high-level meeting on the humanitarian situation in the Horn of Africa. This meeting was well attended, and a number of representatives from various governments and humanitarian organizations joined the discussion. Following an update by Augustine Mahiga, I briefed the participants about the prevailing situation in Somalia. I reported that our government was doing its best with its limited resources to exploit the opportunities presented by the withdrawal of al-Shabaab from the capital and our desire to fill the vacuum with legitimate state authorities.

While describing the mechanisms we had created to deal with the humanitarian crisis, we also assured the participants that my government was committed to implementing the Roadmap in order to end the transition by the August 2012 deadline. I outlined the ongoing efforts in that regard, including progress in drafting a new constitution, formulating a national budget, and establishing transparent and responsive state institutions. I reminded the council that a resource mobilization plan, agreed with international partners, would give some momentum to the peace process, and that a further gathering of a wider group of stakeholders would also be essential.

My mission at the UN once again was to gain support from the international community on the new direction we had taken. I believe I succeeded in that. I saw my presence there as an opportunity not only to network but to tell the international community that the new government meant business, that we were different from previous administrations, and that we wanted Somalia to succeed. We had made commitments, and we had a program and an agenda that would deliver concrete results for Somalia. On the afternoon of September 24, 2011, I delivered a speech to the UN General Assembly (see Appendix B).

The International Contact Group Meeting in Copenhagen

After the conclusion of the UN General Assembly, I proceeded to Copenhagen for the 20th International Contact Group (ICG) meeting on September 29–30. It was the first ICG conference I attended after the Kampala Accord on June 9. I addressed the ICG about the current situation of Somalia, the progress being made, and the future plans of the government.

On the evening of the September 30, I met the U.S. representative for Somalia, Ambassador James Swan. We briefly talked about the relationship between our two countries, how it could be developed further, and how the U.S. government could support the Roadmap. James cared deeply about Somalia and was committed to help the nation succeed. He would soon be visiting the United Arab Emirates, Qatar, and Turkey, and he asked me whether I had any message for the leaders of those countries. I knew I myself would be visiting Qatar and Turkey soon, and thus it was not necessary for me to send messages through James. But I did have a message for the United Arab Emirates: "Stop importing charcoal from Somalia."

The severe drought we were struggling with was a disaster exacerbated by the cutting of trees, which were subsequently sold as charcoal to UAE and, to a lesser extent, to Saudi Arabia. This tree-cutting contributed to the desertification of Somalia. The sad aspect of this is that these offshore consumers of charcoal were mainly using it for recreational purposes while it was detrimentally affecting the lives of so many innocent Somalis.

James reacted positively to my message, and we found a common interest. The main interest of the United States in Somalia has always been the war on terror: Americans knew that al-Shabaab was making a fortune by exporting Somali charcoal from the ports of Kismayo and Barawe. The United States was interested in cutting off this lucrative lifeline for al-Shabaab. At the same time, I was more concerned about the environmental effects in Somalia and the disaster enveloping the country. Thus, we had a mutual interest in stopping the charcoal exports.

Ambassador Swan promised that he would take the message to the government of the UAE. Our respective offices drafted a document for submission to the UN Security Council, we wrote letters to the Security Council, and thankfully our efforts paid off. Within five months, the Security Council issued Resolution 2036, prohibiting the import of charcoal from Somalia. This would not have had happened without the support and commitment of James Swan.

I consider this resolution one of the major achievements of my government. The massive scale of wood-cutting in Somalia was a disaster in the making. If we hadn't done something to stop the trend of exporting millions of sacks of charcoal from Somalia, the nation's environment would have reached a point of no return and the Somali people would eventually have perished. Thank God that did not happen. Today it is illegal to import charcoal from Somalia.

The Garowe 1 Conference

Garowe 1 was a turning point. Prior to this conference, there was very little clarity on how the government of Somalia would accomplish the Roadmap tasks. At Garowe 1, the Roadmap signatories signed the Garowe Principles, which established several important points— that the constitution would be adopted by the NCA instead of by way of a national referendum, that the post-transition Parliament would be bicameral, and that its members would be selected by traditional elders rather than by elections. These were key agreements to clarify the way forward.

We chose to hold constitutional conferences in Garowe for reasons of reconciliation and political outreach. Meeting in Garowe would bring the nation's regional administrations and the TFG closer so that they could together take the country forward. Puntland was at that time the only viable political federal entity in the country supportive of the TFG. We had to reciprocate that goodwill and decided that these important conferences—attended by President Sheikh Sharif, Speaker Shariff Hassan, and the leaders of Galmudug, the ASWJ, and myself—would be held in Puntland.

I had been to Garowe many times before and was familiar with Puntland, but those who were not acquainted with the city were pleasantly surprised. Most of the conference participants were seeing it for the first time, and the parliamentarians, members of civil society, and people coming from all over the country found it to be an unusually peaceful city with no security problems. They were pleased by its calmness and even amused by the lack of artillery shelling and explosions. It seemed remarkable to them that the people of Garowe were walking on the streets in the middle of the night, minding their own business. This was certainly not the situation in southern Somalia.

Holding the conference in Garowe had another symbolic importance. Previous reconciliation conferences held outside

Somalia had often produced undesired results. From now on, we wanted to hold all the conferences in Somalia, in the hope that meeting inside the country would create harmony and closeness between the center and the periphery.

Garowe 1 was an intense meeting. Various groups were discussed different parts of the Roadmap, such as the constitution, parliamentary reform, and good governance institutions. The designated groups met and then presented their recommendations to the Roadmap signatories. It was finally up to the principals to agree. In the end we had to reach consensus.

One of the complex issues was competing ideas concerning the selection of future parliamentarians. Puntland proposed that the future Parliament be based on constituencies, as is the case in most developed countries. Others, particularly the Digil and Mirifle and Dir sub-clans, felt it was advantageous to them to keep the 4.5 formula. The minority clans, on the other hand, disliked the term "4.5" because of its connotation. They felt it was demeaning, as they were told that they basically represented half a clan. However, I believe the 4.5 formula served the minority clans very well and that they fared better in this system. They would not have been elected or selected from any constituency if not for that system, as the quota system reserved seats for them regardless of their minority presence in the country.

Another key issue was the number of the parliamentarians. We initially agreed on 225 members, with 20 percent of them being women. The main features of the Garowe agreement included increasing the role of women in the post-transitional political reality of Somalia. Women were the victims and not the perpetrators of the civil war. They were also the glue that kept Somali society together. Therefore, forsaking them in the post-transition political dispensation would have been unwise and unjust. It was decided to give them a bigger role than they previously had.

Other outcomes in Garowe 1 included a reduction in the size of Parliament and implementing the selection of members on the basis of strict criteria. I addressed the conference about its main priorities and stressed the urgency of the need for change (see Appendix C).

The Garowe 2 Conference

Garowe 2 was held in the capital of Puntland on February 15–17. It was also a critical meeting, and its timing was significant. In Garowe 2, the Roadmap signatories negotiated and agreed on the contentious issues concerning federalism, the status of Mogadishu, and the operationalization of the Garowe Principles (specifying how the National Constituent Assembly [NCA] members and new members of Parliament would be selected). There were whisperings that the international donors wanted to consider an Option B if the Roadmap were to fail. It was therefore critical that Garowe 2 take place the week prior to the London Conference to demonstrate Somalia's resolve in moving forward with the Roadmap.

The main features of Garowe 2 were decisions concerning the electoral system and the federal system, and how representation would work. We introduced an upper house composed of a maximum of fifty-four members, in addition to a lower house. The upper house was representing the federal states, while the lower house represented the population. Many participants in this conference expressed views against the federal system, including even those who were claiming to represent a federal state. For example, Galmudug representatives were against federating Somalia. This was completely counterintuitive: they were against federalism while they themselves claimed to represent a federal state. Mohamed Farah Jimaale said, "We need regional autonomy, not federalism." To me, this was a distinction without a difference. The objectors simply seemed to be reacting to the word "federalism."

Fortunately the principals of the meeting, the Roadmap signatories, worked together and accommodated each other. We had been through so many conferences and meetings together. Sheikh Sharif, who had not wanted to spend a night in Garowe in August, was now comfortable staying there for many days. I am sure he had plenty of goat's milk, a tradition Garowe is known for. Our relationship blossomed there, and our working relations became very positive and productive.

The London Conference

In early July, after I had been appointed prime minister but before the cabinet had been approved by Parliament, I received a call from Nairobi. Matt Baugh, the Commonwealth representative to Somalia, told me that William Hague, the U.K. foreign secretary, would be attending the ceremony marking the independence of South Sudan, and that Hague wanted to meet with me in Nairobi. I had been approved by Parliament on June 28 and thought it would be a good opportunity to talk to Hague and to seek the support of the U.K. government. I met him over a dinner at the British high commissioner's residence in Nairobi. He came across as very open and gregarious, and we discussed many things, including, of course, Somalia, terrorism, al-Shabaab, and the relationship between Somalia and the United Kingdom. He then asked me: "What do you think of Somaliland?"

My answer could have taken me out of the frying pan and put me into the fire. I replied, "Mr. Secretary, in this case my personal opinion doesn't matter. What matters is the policy of the Somali government regarding Somaliland. Our policy is that the sanctity and territorial integrity of Somalia is inviolable. We believe that Somaliland is part and parcel of Somalia. I know they have grievances, I know they have issues with us, and I know it is a very difficult thing to address, but that is the policy of the government. My opinion is a different matter, but I am the prime minister of Somalia, and I can't have a personal opinion in this matter at all."

Having finished my statement, I asked: "Mr. Secretary, what do you yourself think of Somaliland?" He gave me a very diplomatic answer: "I think we are on the same page on this issue."

I'm sure the U.K. government didn't see eye-to-eye with us on this issue, but William Hague didn't express any difference of opinion at the time. I assumed he was just exploring my opinion on the matter and trying to gauge my position. As Somaliland is a former British colony, British diplomats usually have a soft spot for it. That is why, to this day, more than half of U.K. aid to Somalia is intended for Somaliland.

During this meeting, Hague also discussed the British commitment to the progress of Somalia and mentioned the possibility that Britain would hold a conference on Somalia in London. Eventually the

British did hold the conference, and in January 2012, before it began, I paid an official visit to Italy. There I heard the rumor that the London conference had an ulterior motive; that a variety of white papers—Italian, British, and Ugandan—were building scenarios of what to do about Somalia. Whether or not these white papers were authentic, they were creating confusion and uncertainty about the future of Somalia. Rumor had it that if the TFG didn't deliver what it promised and the Roadmap failed, the international community would take ownership of Somalia, and Somalia would be put under UN trusteeship.

The leaders of the TFG—the president, the speaker, and myself—were very apprehensive about what was going to happen in London. We had a number of questions: We had the Roadmap, so why was the London conference being held? What was the reasoning behind it? What would be its outcome? While agreeing that the results of the conference must support the Roadmap and should not be a parallel plan, we said we would not accept any document or communiqué coming out of the London conference that was against the Roadmap. I made our concerns clear at the conference (see Appendix D).

The Istanbul Conference

This Istanbul conference of May 2012 was a follow-up to an earlier Istanbul conference in 2010. After Somalia's devastating drought in 2011, the Turkish government became very committed to the revival of the Somali state and Prime Minister Erdogan promised to ensure that Somalia would have the financial and political backing it needed to end the transition successfully.

Before the conference, I decided to pay an official visit to Turkey. I arrived in Istanbul on May 29, two days before the conference was to commence—and had a fruitful meeting with Prime Minister Erdogan on the night of May 30. He hosted a dinner for the delegation afterward. I had met Erdogan quite a few times before, and I found him very cool and calm. He wanted to gauge me and what we wanted to achieve for Somalia. We discussed a host of subjects, including economics, Somalia, the Roadmap, America, and the West. My opening statement at the Istanbul conference appears in Appendix E.

The Addis Ababa and Nairobi Principals Meetings

To further operationalize the Garowe meetings and move closer toward the NCA, two further meetings were held in Addis Ababa and Nairobi. In May 2012 we traveled to Addis Ababa to sit down with Galmudug, the ASWJ, Puntland, and the other regional stakeholders to finalize the draft constitution. This was done mainly to address any issues these political entities might have regarding the constitution. We appointed a select committee from among the stakeholders to determine whether the draft submitted on April 20, 2012, was satisfactory to all the stakeholders. Needing a document that had universal support, we did not invite the committee of experts because we wanted to create an environment in which people could speak freely.

In Addis Ababa we made some modifications to which all the stakeholders could agree. We had considered our constitution as the most sharia-compliant constitution ever. However, rumors arose that the constitution was not sharia-compliant—that it condoned homosexuality and gay marriage—and spread other misinformation about the constitution. Many Somalis, being part of an oral society with no culture of reading, believed the rumors and the resulting misinformation.

We didn't bow to the naysayers and instead, in early July 2012, we brought the 825 members of the NCA to Mogadishu to show them the final draft of the constitution. We used a creative method: for those who were illiterate or who preferred to hear it, we asked radio personalities to read the constitution out loud so that everyone had an opportunity to fully understand it.

While there was only one official final draft constitution, the critics had produced another copy. When the final draft was taken to a constitutional conference in Nairobi in June 2012, President Sheikh Sharif brought with him an unofficial copy, produced by the detractors. When we arrived at the conference in Nairobi, he said there were competing versions of the constitution. The IFCC, which had been kept as a legal entity, had influenced the committee of experts, particularly the chair, and were delaying the approval process. We took the copy from the IFCC and the committee of experts, and said: "This is it. We have to have a final draft, and this will be it." The minister of constitutional affairs had to take over the process from these two groups in order for us to meet the deadline.

The final copy brought to Nairobi in June 2012 was the one finalized in Addis Ababa in May. Sheikh Sharif and the current speaker Mohamed Jawari stuck to the April 20 version. The president attempted to confuse the gathering and claimed there were two competing versions of the constitution. This was a misleading of the international community and the Somali public to create doubts in the minds of the stakeholders. I responded: "Mr. President, there is only one final draft of the constitution. It's the one we agreed upon in Addis, and this will be the one submitted to the constituent assembly."

Upon returning to Mogadishu from Nairobi, the government launched a wide range of community engagement initiatives, including town hall meetings, to ensure that Somalis weren't misled by the naysayers. An awareness campaign was required so that it would be clear that the constitution was sharia-compliant and that the disinformation was intended to derail the Roadmap process.

THE NATIONAL THEATER BOMBING:

A TURNING POINT

Throughout the years, al-Shabaab had continued its efforts to disrupt the Transitional Federal Government and derail the Roadmap process. It regarded me as the driver of the process, and to stop this it decided in March and April of 2012 to eliminate me. Here is an account of how it almost succeeded.

Usually, the TFG held national security meetings on Sundays and Wednesdays. These meetings were attended by the president, the prime minister, the speaker of Parliament, the ministers of defense, the interior, national security, health, information, and finance, and the commanders of the armed forces (the police, military, and intelligence). They were also sometimes attended by the mayor of Mogadishu.

On March 28, 2012, we held a national security meeting at which the minister of information, Abdulkadir Mohamed Jahweyne, asked all of us, particularly the president and me, to attend a ceremony marking the first anniversary of the re-launch of Somali National Television. We accepted his invitation, but it was still one week down the road, and with all that was going on in Somalia we forgot about it. A day before the event, on April 3, the minister called me and said, "Mr. Prime Minister, tomorrow is the day, and we are counting on you to attend the ceremony."

Like everyone else, I had been preoccupied by state affairs. I apologized for forgetting and thanked him for reminding me. I confirmed that I would attend. I said that the president might have also forgotten, and suggested that the minister call to remind him. The minister did get in touch with the president to inform him that the event would be held the following day. For some reason, the president became annoyed with the minister and said he wouldn't attend. The minister called me and said, "Mr. Prime Minister, the president has said he is not going to come."

I believe the president resented the fact that he wasn't given ownership of the re-launch of Somali TV. I had heard him say, "I invested a lot in this TV station, and now I don't know what's going on." He didn't like the station's management, its independence, or the neutrality of its programs. I can only surmise that he wanted Somali TV to be a mouthpiece for his reelection campaign.

Generally, the president arrived at his office every workday at approximately 10 a.m., but that fateful Wednesday morning he came early. The event was about to begin at around 9 a.m. The minister went to the president to plead with him to attend the event. The president merely replied, "I'm not coming."

I suggested to the minister that if the president couldn't attend he should postpone the entire event for a couple of days, and then try again when the president was calmer. Taking my advice, the minister proposed a postponement, but the president became irate and said, "I'm not coming, and you cannot postpone the event. It has to proceed as scheduled." It was a very strange proposition. This put the minister in a very difficult position—the president was not coming, and the event couldn't be postponed. The minister then came to my residence to tell me what had transpired. I said, "Don't postpone it. My attendance will suffice."

So the minister and I went. By the time we arrived, my security guards were there. They had been there since early morning. I was accompanied by a good number of my cabinet members, including two deputy prime ministers and the ministers of health, information, planning, and international cooperation. It was a very happy occasion, during which we were entertained with emotive national songs by the Waberi Band. An hour or so later, around 11 a.m., I was called to give my keynote speech.

As I walked up to the podium to deliver the speech, I joked with the crowd. I continued to converse with them as I warmed up to my speech. Then, less than five minutes after arriving at the podium, I heard an explosion. I was facing the crowd, and all I could see was flames and dark smoke. It seemed that a bomb had struck and had gone off in the middle of the unsuspecting crowd. I was shocked by the intensity of the explosion.

The scene was complete chaos—death and destruction were everywhere. Almost thirty people were wounded, half of them seriously. The first fatalities were two prominent Somali Olympic officials, Adan Haji Yabarow Wiish and Said Mohamed Noor "Mugamba." Within a couple of minutes, my security people whisked me to my car in a small alley near the theatre and drove me back to my residence.

Less than an hour later, I held a press conference at my residence. I sent condolences to the families who had lost loved ones as a result of this criminal act. I expressed my feeling that this would not deter us from the Roadmap and from saving Somalia; it would not distract us from our goal of a secure and safe nation. I reassured the public that al-Shabaab would not discourage us. I hoped this message would calm the situation and take the country forward. I had to let both the Somali people and the world know that we would keep our eyes on the prize.

Since the president had said that the event could not be postponed and he wasn't coming, there was a rumor that he might have had a hand in the attack. I did not believe it, but it was suspicious behavior, especially to those looking for someone to blame. Moreover, the mayor of the city, the minister of interior and national security, the police chief, and the head of the national intelligence agency were not there either. It was uncharacteristic of them to be missing on such an occasion. That most of those missing were close associates of the president created further suspicion.

Within a few days of the blast, two more people died of injuries sustained during the explosion. One man, Faisal Haji Elmi Amin, was a good friend and staff member who was in charge of the social affairs department of my office. The other fatality was Mowliid Ma'ane Mohamed, an outspoken minister in successive TFG administrations. He had a sharp tongue and never shied away from expressing his views, however controversial they might be.

The suicide bomber was found to be a young female in her early twenties. I believe that this criminal act was perpetrated by al-Shabaab alone. The bombing had the indelible signs of al-Shabaab, a group for whom suicide bombing is a hallmark. There was, however, nothing we as a government could do but persist in pursuing our target.

This was neither the first nor the last time that I would be targeted. I believe in God, and that one can neither postpone nor hasten one's death, so if I died serving my country, there was no better state or condition in which to lose my life. The bombing incident only increased my resolve to protect Somalia from the yoke of al-Shabaab. It also galvanized the country and increased its determination to get rid of this menace. We knew that the enemy would try everything possible to derail the Roadmap.

What was dispiriting was the shoddiness of the investigation and how it was botched. I appointed a cabinet-level committee to investigate the bombing. It was headed by the minister of defense, Hussein Arab Isse, who was also the deputy prime minister. Preoccupied by its daily routine of work, the committee didn't accomplish much. The chief of staff of my office, Abdishakur Mohamud Gurey, tried to undertake his own investigation, but that investigation made things much worse. Abdishakur was working with two detectives, one from the National Security Agency (NSA) and the other from the national police. Abdishakur was somehow convinced that the suicide attack was an inside job and that people in my office had orchestrated it. Half a dozen of my security personnel were put in prison as a result of the two detectives taking advantage of Abdishakur's credulous personality. He was so keen to get to the bottom of the crime that he became susceptible to their manipulation.

The head of the Military Court, General Hassan Mohamed Hussein, "Mungaab," who also served as the Governor of the Benadir region and the Mayor of Mogadishu was a close associate and confidant of President Sheikh Sharif. The general, a distant cousin of the president, was heavily involved in manipulating the investigation to exonerate the president from any possible fallout from this incident. He had no background in law or in the military but was promoted because of clan and loyalty considerations. He wanted to ensure that any judgments would be made in favor of the president.

The investigation's lack of professionalism and competency had an adverse impact on its outcome. I found myself losing faith in the justice system of the very government I was leading. There was no point in asking the president why he hadn't attended the Somali National Theater ceremony; and the bombing's causes are still shrouded in mystery. Within the security apparatus or the government, there must be someone who knows how it could have occurred. Usually, security checks are very tight, and someone must have given the bomber assistance in coming that close to me. Females are checked by two female soldiers, one AMISOM and one Somali. Someone must have facilitated the bomber's passage through all these checkpoints.

The president, meanwhile, was upset with the minister of information, blaming him for the security breaches. A couple of weeks after the incident, the president called me and requested that I fire this minister as well as the minister of planning and international cooperation, Abdullahi Godah Barre. Both men were among the best and the brightest men in the cabinet, and the president gave no reason for his request. I believe he simply resented these ministers' audacity and independence. There was no way I could have fired them and lived with myself. It would have been unconscionable and quite reprehensible.

The president, however, had an unusual perspective: "They are both Hawiye. These are my people, and therefore you have no reason to defend them. If anyone should defend them, it should be me." This was the most outlandish statement I had ever heard. I said, "No, these are two capable, professional ministers, and they do their job very well. Unless you give me a good reason why we should terminate them, I will not do it." The president said, "This will affect

*Prime Minister Abdiweli Mohamed Ali of Somalia meets with
Prime Minister Raila Odinga of Kenya, September 9, 2011 Nairobi*

*Prime Minister Abdiweli Mohamed ALi and Prime Minister Meles
Zenawi of Ethiopia, October 08, 2011 Addis Ababa*

Prime Minister Abdiweli Mohamed Ali with Julio Maria Terzi
Italy's Minister of Foreign Affairs, January 31, 2012 Rome

President Jacob Zuma holds Bilateral talks with recently elected
Somalia Prime Minister Abdiweli Mohamed Ali on the margins of
the 67th United Nations General Assembly September 25, 2012
New York 2012

our relationship." I replied, "So be it. In good conscience, I don't understand why I should fire two of my best cabinet members when they have not committed any crime."

The president resorted to the speaker, Shariff Hassan, to convince me to fire the two ministers. Shariff Hassan came to me and said, "These two cabinet members are not worth the difficulty it creates between you and the president. I think you'd be better off letting them go." I knew Shariff Hassan, and knew that anything he did involved a personal interest, a hidden agenda. He had two people lined up for the job, his close friends, and I knew both men he wanted to fill the positions. I said, "I'm not doing it, sorry."

By now, six or seven of my staff had been in prison for over a month as a result of a conspiracy hatched at the highest level of the government. I was frustrated and finally threatened that I would go public with what I knew. I said this conspiracy by Mungaab and others had to stop. Finally, my staff was released. One of them became very sick in prison, and I remain very angry about how these people were treated. They protected me and were risking their lives for my safety. The way they were treated was abominable.

The work of governing had to continue, but there was no love lost between me and the president. The bombing was a turning point in many ways.

To this day, because the investigation was botched, no one knows exactly who the bomber was or where she came from. We only know that al-Shabaab finally claimed responsibility for the bombing.

FORMING A NEW GOVERNMENT:

THE PARLIAMENTARY ELECTIONS

Selecting the Elders

In March 2012, Somalia's traditional leaders, civil society organizations, and federal leaders including myself attended the burial services of Abdullahi Yusuf, the TFG's first president. After the ceremony, since almost all the stakeholders were present, including President Sheikh Sharif and Speaker Shariff Hassan, we met to discuss the finalization of the constitution and the selection of the members of the National Constituent Assembly (NCA). We saw it as a good opportunity to discuss the way forward.

The mandate of the TFG would soon expire, and a new political dispensation had to be in place by August 2012. The constitution needed to be completed so that the new regime would be constitutionally footed. The 825 members of the NCA had to be brought to Mogadishu to discuss, deliberate, and approve the constitution. That approval would be followed by the selection of the members of Parliament. Then there was the issue of a number of us running for the presidency: the speaker wanted to be president, the president wanted to continue for another term, and I was contemplating running so that I could complete the work I had begun as prime minister. Unfortunately, our political aspirations complicated the discussions and might have created a perception of a conflict of interest.

In that meeting, we decided that 135 elders would be selected— thirty from each of the four main clans, and fifteen from the minority clans. The Garowe Principles stipulated that the signatories would select the NCA members in consultation with civil society and other stakeholders. But we realized that ambitious politicians should not be given a free hand in matters that they could exploit. To avoid any appearance of conflict of interest, we decided that the task of selecting the NCA members as well as the MPs should be delegated to the traditional leaders. This was a huge undertaking, but we felt that the elders were popularly perceived as Somalia's natural leaders. They had in the eyes of many, the moral authority and the natural legitimacy that we politicians lacked, so we were prepared to defer to them in this matter.

This was when my problems with Farole began. Farole at the

time was having issues with Khatumo state of northern Somalia, and most of the genuine traditional leaders of Dhulbahante clan resided in the area claimed by Khatumo. He didn't want Khatumo elders to be given free rein in the selection of the NCA members and future federal MPs; instead, he wanted to single-handedly pick the elders from Puntland in order to influence the selection of MPs and, subsequently, the election of the Somali president. This was unacceptable to me; if I accepted that from Farole, I would have to accept it from everyone else. I didn't want to compromise my standing with other Somalis. If I as a son of Puntland allowed that, how could I tell other Somalis to select their genuine traditional leaders?

Puntland was allocated 17 elders out of the total 135; the Darod had 30, and the southern Darod took 13. Farole, however, sent more than 25 candidates from Puntland to Mogadishu, the majority of who were not genuine elders. I welcomed them but nevertheless had a hard talk with them, informing them that only genuine elders were required and that Puntland could not exceed its quota of 17.

Thus, when the candidate elders showed up in Mogadishu, I accepted those who were genuine and sent away those who weren't— there was no room for them. The Dhulbahante elders, about whom Farole and I had disagreed, showed up to rightfully occupy their four spots. Farole and I continued to haggle, however, over the selection of the elders. He couldn't let it go, the problems continued to fester and he wouldn't accept the way it was.

Another burning issue was the representation of elders from the Isaaq clan, or northern Dir, hailing from Somaliland. The genuine traditional leaders of Somaliland were not able to come because they were in the Guurti, the elders' council of Somaliland. Therefore, for Somaliland we had to come up with a novel approach, a new idea of how to have them represented. We decided to contact proxy elders and asked them to obtain an approval for their representative role from their traditional leaders in Somaliland. They did so, and fortunately as a result Somaliland too was represented in the political process in Mogadishu.

The Swearing-in of the New Parliament

The swearing-in of the new Parliament almost did not take place because of security threats and much last-minute bargaining. What would have had happened if August 20, 2012, had passed without a new Parliament being sworn in? First, the mandate of the government would have expired and the existing institutions would have lacked any legitimacy. Second, the country would have been plunged into a new political crisis. If the mandate of the TFG had expired without a new political dispensation in place, a power vacuum would have been created, leading to a political crisis with massive and negative security implications.

Nevertheless, while very aware of this, some spoilers of the Roadmap process decided to try to prevent the swearing-in of the new Parliament. The ceremony was scheduled to take place at the National Police Academy, which had been renovated to host events such as these. The minister of the interior and the commander of the Somali police force created unnecessary obstacles by insisting that the event to be held at the academy. Their sole purpose was to derail the Roadmap and push Somalia to the edge. These elements were pushing the agenda of some senior officials who vehemently opposed the completion of the Roadmap.

They wrongly believed that the international community would never allow a power vacuum in Somalia and would therefore extend the TFG mandate for at least one additional year. Eventually, however, the swearing-in ceremony did take place, on the parking lot of the Mogadishu airport, at dusk on August 20. As the sun set, the new parliamentarians were sworn in, ten at a time. The major hurdles had been overcome and Somalia had a renewed Parliament.

Preparing for the Presidential Elections

Before becoming prime minister, I had served in my predecessor's cabinet as the minister of planning and international cooperation. Now I was ready to move up a notch and decided to run for the presidency. I believed I was in a position to take Somalia forward. I thought that Somalia needed a leader with a vision—someone with political imagination, someone who could create institutions that would guide the country politically, socially, and economically. I wanted to ensure that the hard-won fruits of the Roadmap would not be wasted.

The sitting president, Sheikh Sharif, had also decided to run. Thinking I would pose a serious challenge, he proposed that I support him for the presidency and that I stay on as prime minister. I did not think Sheikh Sharif was the right person for the presidency; neither did I consider his proposal to me an attractive one. Furthermore, the entire year I was in office, the president and I had a merely formal relationship—we didn't always see eye to eye, and I believed that many of the things he had done toward the end of the year were damaging to the institutions of government. For example, he had tried to single-handedly create fifty-six additional districts within the span of three months, from May to August of 2012, merely to win votes. He had promoted thirty-four colonels, all at once, to the rank of general, making me wonder, Where are the troops for these generals? Sheikh Sharif had done all of this without the approval of the cabinet, which was mandated to oversee Somalia's administrative, political, and economic matters.

Initially, around twenty-five candidates announced their intention to run for the presidency. The bar was so low that almost anyone could enter the race. Shariff Hassan, the speaker of the house, also announced his desire to run. He was facing a challenge, however: another member of the Digil and Mirifle clan was running for the speaker position. According to the 4.5 power-sharing arrangement, if a Digil and Mirifle member became speaker, Shariff Hassan would not be eligible to run for the presidency. So, to make his case, he proclaimed that this was the time for the Digil and Mirifle, who had never had a member assume the presidency or the premiership, to move up a notch.

There was a kernel of truth in this assertion, but there was also more than that: Shariff Hassan was promoting his personal and parochial interest. To further this, he tried to find candidates from the Darod, Hawiye, and Dir clan groups who would vie for the speaker position. According to the unwritten rules of clan balance I, as a Darod, would not be able to run for either the presidency or the prime ministership if another Darod became the speaker. Thus, Shariff Hassan's political mischief was running counter to my political ambitions. He then asked me whether I would be able to help him find a Hawiye candidate for the speakership, so that Sheikh Sharif would not be eligible to run. I replied that I didn't support him on this issue. I did not want to be involved in these tactics.

Eventually he found a credible candidate for the speaker position in Ali Khalif. Ali, a former prime minister and minister in the Siad Barre government, had a wealth of political experience and was also a professor of public administration. However, since he hailed from the Dhulbahante sub-clan of my Darod clan family, I was in for a fight. If Ali became the speaker, my entire campaign would come to a screeching halt. My prospects of running for the presidency hinged on finding a suitable non-Darod candidate who could defeat Ali in the race for the speakership. I did not have to look far.

I was fortunate to find Mohamed Sheikh Osman Jawari, from the Digil and Mirifle clan. Like Ali Khalif, he had a wealth of administrative and political experience. He had served under Siad Barre as the minister of labor and sports and was the chairman of the committee of experts I had appointed in September 2011 to speed up the process of finalizing the constitution. However, the speaker must be an MP first, and to thwart this requirement Shariff Hassan tried to block Jawari from membership in Parliament. When that did not succeed, he tried to convince Jawari not to vie for the position. The two men had never been on good terms, but now Jawari felt that Shariff Hassan was abusing the dignity of the Digil and Mirifle.

Jawari wasn't my preferred candidate; I preferred Mohamed Rashid, a former accountant general, who was also a Digil and Mirifle MP. We were very close, but many MPs felt that he was too weak a candidate and not as credible as Jawari. Furthermore, there was an excitement about Jawari in Parliament, and many welcomed the news of his candidacy.

The Parliamentary Split

Shariff Hassan's management style offended many people. When he was the speaker, Parliament was completely dysfunctional; in fact, during my tenure as prime minister, there was no sitting Parliament. Many people attribute that failure to Shariff Hassan. When the MPs voted him out he refused to leave, and Parliament was split between those who supported him and those who were against him. Nevertheless, the president and I supported him, because the Kampala Accord dictated that we should work in a spirit of mutual respect and collegiality. It stipulated that there would be no impeachment of either the president or the speaker. Furthermore, Shariff Hassan was cooperative in supporting the Roadmap. I believe he was more supportive of the Roadmap than was the president himself. Moreover, if I supported his ouster, I would have no control over who the next speaker might be. I could work with Shariff Hassan so long as he supported the process. The unfortunate result of my supporting him was that many MPs who were against Shariff Hassan also harbored animosity toward me. However, the very Parliament that was trying to oust him had also overwhelmingly approved the Kampala Accord, which was clear on the issue of impeachment: there was no reason to dismiss him so long as he was supportive of the Roadmap. The process of moving Somalia forward superseded my personal feelings there. Also, Parliament was completely unruly and thus a threat to the administration, and its dysfunctionality ironically served us very well. As there were no sessions of Parliament, there were no motions against the government, at least during that year.

On the evening of August 22, 2012, I brought Mohamed Rashid and Jawari, together with their supporters, to my office. The group included eighteen Digil and Mirifle MPs under the tutelage of Fawzia Mohamed Sheikh, the main backer of both men. The Digil and Mirifle had a total of sixty-one seats in Parliament, so her group was a substantial part of that. Fawzia is an astute politician and a very shrewd person. She was very loyal to me and had supported me from the beginning. At the same time, she did want not to encourage any possibility that Shariff Hassan might return as the leader of the Digil and Mirifle. She believed that he was not a full-blooded Digil and Mirifle but belonged to a minority Ashraf clan and was related to the Digil and Mirifle through his maternal uncles.

The Lisan sub-clan, of which Shariff Hassan's maternal uncles are members, is a formidable group within the Digil and Mirifle. Thus, many in the clan resented the fact that a minority representative among them had a great deal of control over their politics. Both Fawzia and Jawari hail from the Elay sub-clan of the Digil and Mirifle clan family. Mainly concentrated in Burhakaba, they are considered the largest of the Digil and Mirifle sub-clans. To them, Shariff Hassan's domination of their politics was unacceptable.

This was clan politics at its worst, and it was epitomized by Shariff Hassan and associates.

When I brought Mohamed Rashid and Jawari to my office, I asked Mohamed Rashid to withdraw his candidacy and support Jawari. Otherwise, the Digil and Mirifle votes would be divided and the risk of both men losing to Ali Khalif would be very high. If, on the other hand, we all supported Jawari, there was a high probability that he would win the speakership. It did not guarantee a shoe-in, but it bettered the odds of winning. Fortunately, Mohamed Rashid accepted my proposal and withdrew his candidacy.

Ultimately Jawari managed to become an MP and then to run for the speakership. On August 28, when the votes were cast, he was the leading candidate, gaining over ninety votes. He eventually won, after Ali Khalif conceded and withdrew his candidacy before the second round of voting was announced.

The Presidential Race

My wife Hodan, who all this while had remained in the United States, teaching at the State University of New York at Buffalo, now joined me in Mogadishu and did her best to support my candidacy. She organized women's groups and shared her political observations with me. Hodan has a critical eye and could share insights and opinions with me that others were unable or unwilling to share, and that was very important. She stayed throughout the campaign period and left to return to her teaching job only one day before the election.

Mogadishu was buzzing with all the candidates' campaigns and slogans. This was the biggest event in Somalia in the past forty years—a presidential election, a parliamentary election inside Somalia, for the first time since 1969. It was also a security challenge. There was the constant threat that al-Shabaab could strike at any time, particularly on Election Day. And there were the recurring economic challenges to the government. Holding an election is costly, and the international community did not provide much in the way of financial assistance. We felt as though the world was setting us up for failure. It was a real surprise to many in the international community that Somalis succeeded in holding these elections. However, we succeeded, and were delayed by only 20 days.

In the short period of democracy that Somalia had enjoyed half a century earlier, between 1960 and 1969, citizens had cast the votes for their representatives in Parliament. The MPs, in turn, had voted for the president. Somalia had never had direct democracy, in that it had never held a general election for the president. Rather, it had a parliamentary president instead of a popular president. The situation was similar in 2012, the difference now being that MPs were not elected by the people but selected by the traditional leaders.

Ultimately, though, the MPs voted not according to the presidential speeches or debates. The election was determined by regionalism, clannism, and religious allegiances, and ultimately the man with the most money won the election. As mentioned later in the UN's Somalia and Eritrea monitoring group report of 2013, much money changed hands and the election was tainted by corruption.

The following table shows how the parliamentary votes were cast for the primary presidential candidates.

First Round	Second Round
Sheikh Sharif: 64	Hassan Sheikh: 191
Hassan Sheikh: 60	Sheikh Sharif: 84
Abdiweli Ali: 30	

Why did I lose the election, after so many positive accomplishments in the span of a year or so? There are several reasons why I came short, but I will elucidate some that I consider pivotal. First, I was not targeting any of the candidates and was not involved in the selection of MPs. We had the Technical Selection Committee (TSC) for that purpose, and I decided to adhere to the committee's decision, whereas the president and the speaker were heavily involved in the selection process. All those accused of being warlords, and all the women the TSC considered to have no good moral compass, were now supporters of Sheikh Sharif. He advocated for them and they voted for him, and I might say deservedly so. Many thought I was working with the TSC and that it was taking its cues from me. I was completely oblivious to this suspicion.

Sheikh Sharif, however, was a maverick and shrewd enough to champion the cause of these warlords and the women identified by the TSC, and this gained him votes. On the other hand, I lost all twenty votes from these groups, plus their supporters—and they had many supporters in Parliament. The current president, Hassan Sheikh, was also against the warlords, but he managed to secure sixty votes, which was enough to proceed to the second round of voting. He was not then considered a threat to anyone, and no one thought he had a chance of success.

Second, I spent a great deal of time trying to secure the forty-five votes of the northern Dir. Unlike the situation in previous elections, the government of Somaliland became very much involved in this election because it had a vested interest in deciding who became president. It was adamantly opposed to any Darod becoming the president of Somalia because it felt that a Darod would not be sympathetic to Somaliland's secessionist ambitions.

It appeared that for ideological reasons they had decided to ensure that I would not become president. So, even though I invested a great deal of time and energy into getting the bloc vote of the the northern Dir, I couldn't muster it for political and clan reasons.

A no less important reason for why I lost is the way we handled the Digil and Mirifle, including Fawzia Mohamed Sheikh and her group. At first, they supported me. We had many discussions and worked together for Jawari's success. This was a formidable block, which opposed the Machiavellian politics of Shariff Hassan and supported the ongoing political process to move the country forward.

In this midst of all this, some of my supporters in Kenya invited Shariff Hassan to meet them in Nairobi. They were under the impression that he might help my candidacy and have some influence on these seventy-six votes. This situation caused me a great deal of inconvenience. When the news leaked, Fawzia and her group thought I was sleeping with the devil. They thought I had switched allegiances and was warming up to Shariff Hassan. This was not the case at all; I didn't even know he was traveling to Nairobi.

I told them that this was a mistake, that what those supporters had done was wrong. They felt otherwise, and as a result Fawzia and her group pulled their support from me and decided to back the current president, Hassan Sheikh. Unfortunately, while I lost this group's support, I did not in doing so gain the support of Shariff

Hassan's group. When he traveled to Kenya, he made promises that he would support me. However, he subsequently visited supporters of Sheikh Sharif in Dubai, where I suspect that money changed hands and Shariff Hassan was paid to support Sheikh Sharif. At the last minute, Sheikh Sharif and Shariff Hassan had a meeting at City Plaza Hotel in Mogadishu, where Shariff Hassan declared his support for Sheikh Sharif. I am not sure whether that helped or hurt Sheikh Sharif's candidacy. Many MPs thought "the disliked duo" was returning, and that did not please all of them.

Shariff Hassan had once told me, "If I do not become president, the next best person would be Sheikh Sharif." I asked him why, and he replied, "Whatever I asked of him, he never said no." And that was always the case; Shariff Hassan always had some sort of spell over Sheikh Sharif.

Perhaps the final reason I lost the election had to do with my relationship with my cabinet. Sometimes an asset can at times become a liability. I had a good relationship with my ministers, and those MPs vying for ministerial positions assumed that if I won the presidency I would reinstate the previous cabinet. They might have thought, Abdiweli has his own team, so why should I vote for him? Thus the Ogaden, or Hawadle, or Lelkase MPs would not vote for me because people of their clan or sub-clan already occupied positions in my cabinet and they saw no further reason to support me. Having loyal friends—which should have been an asset for me—may have been a liability in the end.

I had lost the support of the three large groups mentioned above, and as a result my candidacy appeared to be doomed. I received thirty votes in the first round, which was not sufficient. I felt I could not get enough votes to win if that was all I was starting out with. I began to understand the various issues that hampered my presidential bid in the following days, weeks, and months. Although Hassan Sheikh did not appear to be a formidable candidate at first, I can think of three reasons why he won. One was the Somaliland factor: the MPs from Somaliland made conscious decisions to defeat any Darod candidate, and as a result Hassan Sheikh received votes from the northern Dir. Second, a large number of Digil and Mirifle who initially supported me shifted their votes in his favor. Finally, I believe that Hassan Sheikh had more money, which many say came from Qatar.

Late one night, while the campaign was in high gear, Hassan Sheikh came by my office. The rumor mill was in full swing that I was the leading candidate. He said, "Abdiweli, if you support me in my bid for the presidency, I will keep you on as prime minister." At that time he was an unknown, so I thought this was a strange proposal. I replied, "Hassan, I am the current sitting prime minister, and you are without influence. Why should I defer to you, support your bid, and settle for being prime minister? I have the advantage of incumbency, and I think I have more of a chance—so why should I hand the contest over to you?"

His answer was stunning: "Abdiweli, this is Mogadishu, the Hawiye stronghold. All I want is to protect you from the problems of the Hawiye." I replied, "Hassan, this is not the Hawiye stronghold. Rather, it is the capital of Somalia, and I am the prime minister of Somalia. I don't believe the nonsense that this is a Hawiye city and that therefore I will have problems with the Hawiye if I become president. We are all Somalis ultimately." He suggested that we should still support each other; we shook hands, and I wished him good luck. That is why I supported him when I came short.

There was a definite perception that Mogadishu would be in flames if a Darod became president. Many MPs believed that they would not be able to work in Mogadishu if they elected a Darod. That perception was complete nonsense. When I announced that I would withdraw my candidacy before the second round of voting, I told people to support change. That meant voting for Hassan Sheikh, not for Sheikh Sharif.

President Obama (R) Prime Minister Abdiweli Mohamed Ali (2nd Right) First Lady Michelle Obama and Dr. Hodan Isse (R) wife of PM Ali September 21, 2011 United Nations, New York

President of Somalia Sheikh Sharif Ahmed (C) talks as President of Kenya Mwai Kibaki (L) and Prime Minister of Somalia Abdiweli Mohamed Ali listen on during the Somalia Conference at Lancaster House February 23, 2012 London

Prime Minister Abdiweli Mohamed Ali, on the left, and Jose Manuel Barroso President of the European Commission February 21, 2012 Brussels, Press Conference

Prime Minister Abdiweli Mohamed Ali of Somalia and Prime Minister Raila Odinga of Kenya September 9, 2011 Nairobi

The retelling of how the internal mechanisms of the Somali political process functions serves a dual purpose. First, it highlights the deficiencies of the system now known as the 4.5 system. This formula allots government positions on the basis of one position for each so-called large clans/clan families and one half for all so-called minorities.. Winning elections in such an environment becomes a dirty business, shaped by horse-trading under the table. Second, it places under the microscope the shortsighted way in which decisions are made and executed in our political process. Alliances are built on quicksand, and there are no long-term objectives or strategies prepared. Becoming a President, Prime Minister or a Minister as a goal in itself is the be all and end all.

At the time of the elections a group known as Group 16, composed of all the candidates except Shariff Hassan, Sheikh Sharif, and me, formed as a coalition against the incumbents. However, although they tried to form an alliance against us, they could not agree on a single alternative candidate. Of the three frontrunners—Hassan Sheikh, Ahmed Samatar, and Abdirahman Badiyow—none was willing to withdraw and nominate one of the others as a sole candidate. The only way they could win was to agree on a sole candidate, but they could not do that.

I was sure that I would not seek the position of prime minister again because I felt I had a very clear vision of where Somalia should be heading economically, socially and politically. I was running for the presidency, and Hassan Sheikh also didn't feel comfortable with my being prime minister. He felt I would be too strong and too independent, as I had been with Sheikh Sharif.

MATTERS OF STATE:

THREATS MET AND OBSTACLES OVERCOME

Al-Shabaab's Attack on the President

Kenya, as Somalia's neighbor, has always been interested in the peace and reconciliation process in Somalia, so much so that when the TFG was established in 2004, it occurred in Mbagathi, Kenya, after a difficult two-year process. So it was not surprising that in 2012, two days after Hassan Sheikh Mohamud had been sworn in as the president of Somalia, a delegation from Kenya, headed by Sam Ongeri, that country's minister of foreign affairs, arrived in Mogadishu to congratulate the new president and commend us on the timely conclusion of the Roadmap.

The delegation visited the president at the Jazeera Hotel on September 12. When the Kenyan foreign minister arrived, Hassan Sheikh asked me to attend the meeting. He had not yet nominated a new prime minister, and as such I was serving as the caretaker prime minister. Moreover, I had a cordial relationship with the Kenyan government.

The president's security had been taken over by AMISOM, yet there was some confusion over the issue of responsibility. Taking advantage of this confusion, some al-Shabaab members managed to obtain Somali military uniforms and were hanging around at the hotel when the officials arrived. No one questioned their presence or suspected them of being impostors.

When I arrived I was accompanied by my own security detail, which had the same uniform as the al-Shabaab infiltrators. AMISOM thought the impostors were part of my detail, while my security guards thought they were part of the president's detail. When the Kenyan delegation arrived, we proceeded to the second floor of the hotel. We were in the midst of discussions, and the foreign minister and the president were preparing to make a joint press statement, when the head of my security detail sensed that something was wrong. He didn't feel comfortable with the men outside the hotel and became suspicious about the situation.

He sent another one of my security guards, a young man

Abdihakim Hashi Mohamed nicknamed "African," downstairs to see what was going on. As "African" was leaving the building, he saw one of the suspicious men walk into it. He stopped the man and asked him who he was. The man shouted "Allahu Akbar" and blew himself up. "African" died instantly. If it weren't for "African's" intervention, many more innocent people would have died.

There were three attackers that day. The second attacker tried to take advantage of the explosion by running into the building, but AMISOM shot him dead. A third man, who had been waiting outside the gate, tried to run into the compound and was shot by my security personnel.

It was unnerving, but it was Mogadishu. We had to continue the work and prepare the press statement. We were safe, but tragically "African" and others lost their lives in protecting us.

Revisiting the UN General Assembly

A few days after al-Shabaab's attack, the president asked me to attend the UN General Assembly. He felt he needed more time to familiarize himself with the situation in Mogadishu and to deal with the new government and the search for a new prime minister. I was pleased to accept his invitation.

When I arrived in New York, it seemed the whole world had come to the United Nations to welcome Somalia. There was enthusiasm about the change in government, about the fact that Somalia had delivered on the Roadmap, that there was a new Parliament, a new constitution, and a new political dispensation in place. It often seemed to me that out of nowhere a dignitary would come up and ask if I was the Somali prime minister, and then congratulate me.

I thought, here is euphoria of which the government of Somalia can take advantage. The new government had started on a good footing, with internal legitimacy based on the elections, which in turn gave it credibility with the international community. On September 20, 2012, I stressed the nation's bright prospects in my remarks to the UN General Assembly (see Appendix F).

I returned to Somalia in late September, hopeful about the country's future. That was how the new government came into the picture. The president had to nominate a prime minister within 30 days, and when that nomination was approved by Parliament, the prime minister had 30 days in which to appoint a cabinet.

As mentioned earlier, I had run for president and lost, and I wasn't interested in being prime minister again. I was planning to return to the United States to join my family in Buffalo, New York, and resume teaching. There was, however, a complication: the elders of Galkayo had selected me as an MP in the new Parliament, and I needed to travel to Puntland to consult with those I was supposed to be representing. I wanted to discuss my goals and desires for the future with them, but before doing that I had to wait for a new prime minister to be appointed. The appointee turned out to be none other than my good friend Abdi Farah Shirdon. He was approved by Parliament on October 17.

I gave Shirdon advice on a few issues after he had been appointed prime minister, but I generally kept my distance so that he could discharge his duties without undue influence. For example, he asked for advice on the size of the cabinet. I advised him to make his cabinet between 23 and 27 members because we needed reconciliation among Somalis, and therefore the cabinet needed to reflect all of Somalia. It needed to be a cabinet that all Somalis could see themselves in; therefore, no less than 23, but no more than 27.

I later discovered that the president had a different view, and the prime minister reduced the number of ministries from 18 to 10. To me, reducing the number of ministries made no sense. It created a huge burden for those in charge. For example, the ministries of education, health, social services, and women's affairs were all combined in one ministry. It would be very difficult for one person to manage all these portfolios and to give each ministry the attention it deserved. There is a place for a small and efficient government, but it is also possible to be too small to perform effectively.

My Visit to Puntland

On October 18, I left Mogadishu to touch base with my constituency in Puntland. Not only is it the place where my constituents resided, but Puntland is also my birthplace and the place where my umbilical cord is buried. I planned to stay in and travel around the region for a month.

I arrived in Galkayo and received an unforgettable reception, an amazing welcome from both the people and the administration, including the governor and other officials of the Mudug region. They congratulated me on the good work I had done, and I was happy to see that they were clearly proud of their native son. I then met my traditional leader, Islan Bashir, to discuss the future of Puntland. I remained in Galkayo for a few days, talking to people, gauging their views on the way forward for Somalia and their understanding of the situation in Puntland. They were concerned about the economy and politics of Puntland, and I heard about their dire situation. Then I headed to Galdogob, a district west of Galkayo.

On my way to Galdogob, I stopped at Hero Jale, a village mainly populated by a minority group who is shunned by the major clans. The village has no hospitals and no schools, and the people of Hero Jale are resigned to the fact that they are considered inferior. They are considered outcasts and are called by such derogatory names as Midgan and Tumaal. But these people are Somalis, they are Muslims, and they have a stake in the country too. It is unacceptable to treat them as they are treated, and visiting them touched me deeply. One of their sayings is "Even the lorries, cars, and trucks don't stop in this village." When they spoke to me about their plight, I looked around and saw youngsters listening too. I felt deeply uncomfortable; imagine a child listening to a conversation about the mistreatment faced by his family.

Somalia is a society whose socioeconomic base is livestock. Historically these people, the outcasts, were deprived of the ownership of livestock, so they resorted to other livelihoods such as hunting, welding, and shoemaking. It is ironic that in Somalia the technically accomplished trades of welding and shoemaking are considered inferior to pastoralism.

This issue is not peculiar to Somalia; in other areas, it is much worse. But it is the most difficult social problem Somalia faces today, and something has to be done to give marginalized people their due. They don't demand change, but just ask for it, because they are resigned to their situation. Their children, as a result, have low self-esteem. They don't go to school, even in the larger cities, because they are told: "Why try? You are a midgan anyway." They don't look for jobs or try to "improve" themselves. They are often damaged emotionally and thus are completely disenfranchised.

The visit to Hero Jale was an eye-opener for me. What I saw was racism at its worst. I don't think this issue is being seriously discussed by Somalis; we need a new debate on it. I told the people of Hero Jale I would try my best and that I would advocate for them to get a school and a clinic.

Then I arrived in Galdogob to meet with the elders of the city. The last time I had visited was 1975, during a drought, when most of my nomadic family had lost their livestock. They had become internally displaced in Galdogob, which was why I visited the city then. The city had been a village in 1975, but now it was a metropolitan center with all the amenities of modernity, including water, electricity, and telephones. An election was intended to be held in Puntland within a few months, and although that did not occur I met with the elders and again discussed events in Somalia in general and Puntland in particular.

I then travelled to other parts of Puntland, visiting all the cities between Galkayo and Garowe, the seat of the government of Puntland, and arrived in Garowe on October 24. My relationship with President Abdirahman Mohamed Farole was not an easy one— he wasn't sure what to expect from me and was apprehensive about my presence in Puntland—so when I met him in Garowe, I told him I was in Puntland to visit my family and engage with my constituency. I assured him that I was not there to muddy the political waters or stir up trouble.

I had no hard feelings towards the Farole I considered what had happened between us as over and done with. I I had let it go and forgotten about it, and I was expecting the same attitude from him. The next day was the Eid-ul-Adha celebration, one of the most important dates on the Islamic calendar. That morning, the president Farole and I prayed together at the big mosque and talked to the people of Garowe. It was a happy occasion. After prayers, I proceeded with my journey to the city of Qardo. It is a city close to my heart, as it is where my beloved wife, Hodan, was born and my brother-in-law, Mohamed Said, was then the mayor.

When I arrived in Qardo on October 26, many people came

out to give me a warm welcome. I think my brother-in-law had
something to do with this. I spent a couple of days there visiting
the landmarks of the city, including schools and hospitals. Qardo is
mainly populated by the Osman Mohamud sub-clan, which derives
from the kingdom of Osman Mohamud. Its members are considered
a clan aristocracy and the leaders of the Darod. I stayed there for
two days, hearing a multitude of complaints about how Puntland
was deteriorating economically, socially, and politically. The people
I heard from were disenchanted with the current leadership and felt
that Puntland needed a new direction and a change of leadership.
These views were widely held.

This was when I experienced a tectonic shift in my interest—
from considering Puntland in the context of the federal Parliament to
considering the issues within Puntland itself. Many people I spoke
with in my travels around Puntland encouraged me to stay put and
remain there.

President Farole had wanted me to conclude my visit in Qardo
and not go to Bosaso, but I simply couldn't disregard Bosaso. It is
the biggest city in Puntland and the commercial center of the state.
I traveled there on October 29. Farole didn't like the reception I
had received in Qardo, or in Puntland overall, for that matter, and
instructed the authorities in Bosaso to keep people away from me.
Despite this, the residents of Bosaso came out in their thousands
to greet me. The governor, the mayor, and the chief of the armed
forces met me outside the city and told me they would take me to
the official guesthouse. I refused, feeling that if I accepted their
offer they would have control of who came to visit me, and that was
unacceptable.

As a result, they brought me to the residence designated by my
advance team. Unfortunately, and unknown to me, this was a house
owned by one of Farole's fierce opponents, Liban Musse Boqor.
Farole and his people took it as an offense, and when the governor,
mayor, and chief of the armed forces realized the house belonged
to Liban Musse Boqor they handed me a letter listing the names of
twelve people. They said, "Prime Minister, we don't want you to see
these twelve people. They are troublemakers."

I was not familiar with any of the names and replied, "I don't know these twelve people. I don't know who they are or what they look like. If they are guilty of a crime, you can arrest them and take them to prison. But if someone comes to my door, I cannot question them and check to see if they are on this list. I will receive whoever comes to my door, whether they are critical of or loyal to the state." I could not refuse to see people just because Farole disliked them. Eventually my escorts agreed and left the house.

Now I was exhausted. I hadn't slept well in the previous few nights, so I went to my room and fell asleep immediately. I woke up at 6 p.m., when the people accompanying me announced: "The house is surrounded." Farole had ordered the army to surround the house and keep people from visiting me. It was almost like a house arrest; a complete battalion surrounded the house. They prevented a couple of ministers from visiting me, including Sayid Mohamed Abdulle Hassan, the state minister for planning and international cooperation, even though they knew who he was. They even refused to let the cook enter the house, and I didn't eat dinner that evening.

I telephoned Farole. He didn't pick up the phone. He knew my telephone number but apparently ignored my calls. Then I decided to call one of his closest associates, Ali Yusuf Ali Hosh, the deputy minister of the interior. He was one of a group of about twelve people referred to as Aranjan, "the devil's associates," essentially Farole's elite squad. They were very influential, more powerful than Farole's ministers, and were essentially his kitchen cabinet.

Ali answered immediately. I said, "Ali, I know that you know what's going on in Bosaso. Tell me, why the brute force? And why are you surrounding the house with military personnel?" I also told him that I had called the president and that he had refused to answer the phone. Ali said that the president was probably busy or otherwise engaged and said that he would check. A few minutes later he called back. What he didn't tell me was that Farole's son Mohamed was listening in on our conversation.

Midway through the conversation, Farole's son interrupted. I had been speaking freely, and on being made aware of the eavesdropping I found his listening-in disconcerting and uncalled for. Mohamed Farole tried to tell me that the 'security presence' was for my own protection, because the city was full of al-Shabaab operatives. I replied that I had thirty well-armed guards and didn't need more protection. I demanded that the army immediately vacate the property.

I believe Mohamed and Ali then had discussions with Farole. Soon our disagreement became public, and many people were angry on my behalf. Early the next morning, the military was removed from the premises. Immediately I started to receive visitors, and forty-two people came to see me within a few minutes of the army's departure. The most prominent residents of Bosaso—businessmen, traditional leaders, religious leaders, former civil servants—were among them, as were the twelve "forbidden" people on the list. I found that these twelve were prominent citizens, and one was even a former minister.

The visitors carped about matters of state. They said Puntland had become a police state and that they were not free to talk or even gather publicly. They told me that they had once tried to hold a lunch gathering of traditional elders in Bosaso but that the police had removed them from the gathering place, locked the rooms, and confiscated their laptops and other personal belongings.

Although I could not verify all the accusations, this visit was eye-opening. Every time I had visited Puntland in the past, I had been surrounded by Farole and his group. Clearly I had not fully understood the situation. Farole was told immediately about my visitors, and that evening the deputy minister of finance, Abdirahman Mohamud Haji Hassan, said that Farole wanted to talk to me. I replied that I didn't want to talk to Farole anymore. But Abdirahman eventually convinced me to speak to Farole, and when I did, he said, "You have seen enough in the two days you have been in Bosaso. I want you to leave Bosaso immediately."

I replied, "Bosaso doesn't belong to anybody. It is as much my constituency as it is yours, and no one can force me to leave. I will leave Bosaso on my own terms, when my work is done."

Now Farole was fuming. There was no further discussion to be had. I had planned to visit some schools, but the visits were cancelled, probably by the governor or the mayor. I decided to leave. The next morning, the governor called and asked me to visit, saying he needed to talk to me. I went to his office and saw that the minister of livestock, Said Hassan Shire, was also there. He didn't appear to like the treatment I was getting in Bosaso either.

The governor said that he knew I was well liked and respected, but at the end of the day they followed the orders of the president of Puntland, and I should leave the city. I repeated that I would not leave until I was done. Nevertheless I left the city the next morning, not because I was forced to but because my mission in Bosaso was done. I had wanted to visit Badhan, but one of the traditional elders told me that the area was unsafe: I could be assassinated there by anyone, but it would be blamed on al-Shabaab. Since I had met most of the elders of Badhan in Bosaso, I decided to return to Galkayo.

I stopped in Garowe to visit Farole's traditional elder, Islan Isse. I didn't visit him to complain, but out of respect, and we talked for an hour on issues related to Puntland. Islan Isse was dismayed by Farole's behavior. At that time, Farole wasn't in Garowe but in a small city called Jalam, and I was told that he was waiting to see me there. I didn't know what his intentions were, but I had no reason to see him and I declined to visit him.

Back in Galkayo, on November 5, I issued a press statement about what I had seen and what had been said to me. I considered the statement fair and balanced and made no mention of my mistreatment. What I did say was a summary of what the people had told me they were concerned about: the lack of social services, the lack of infrastructure, the lack of freedom of the press and of opinion, and the fragile peace and security of Puntland. Looming large among their fears was the apprehension they felt about the disintegration of their state—as had occurred in the case of Khatumo state—mainly because of Farole's dangerous policies. Essentially I tried to become a voice for the voiceless of Puntland.

The next day, Puntland's minister of information responded by accusing me of destabilizing Puntland and of not doing enough for it during my tenure as prime minister of Somalia. He said I had neglected Puntland and failed to encourage development projects there. It was a baseless accusation: Puntland received its fair share in the sixteen months that I was prime minister. Moreover, my duty was to be fair to all of Somalia, regardless of my clan connections to Puntland. I was the prime minister of Somalia, not the prime minister of Puntland.

Relations with Puntland during my Tenure as Prime Minister

When I became prime minister of Somalia in 2011, Puntland was considered a hub of piracy. Some in the international community believed that President Farole and his ministers were involved in piracy—a UN monitoring group report made the allegation, implicating the president as well as the minister of the interior and the minister of national security. Ayl, the president's clan base, was a piracy hub, and the president was accused of receiving campaign funds from pirates.

I had asked the international community to provide peaceful areas of Somalia such as Puntland and Somaliland with development projects, because these areas didn't really require humanitarian services. When I was in Nairobi, I spoke to a senior representative of the international community there and asked if they could start with one or two projects. He asked what kind of projects might help Puntland. I replied that the most important and urgent project was to repave the road between Galkayo and Garowe. This road, the lifeline of Puntland, was relatively good between Garowe and Bosaso but bad between Garowe and Galkayo.

I provided a damage assessment conducted by the EU in 2000. The representative said he had met Farole, who did not consider that road a priority but instead asked them to invest the money in building a road between Ayl and Garowe. The representative then added derisively, "Do you know why Farole is interested in building the road between Ayl and Garowe? He wants a fast track for his piracy business."

I was annoyed that Puntland had that negative image. I replied, "The president of Puntland is not a pirate and is not involved in the piracy business. Puntland is not just about piracy; it is a peaceful area which of course has a piracy problem, but that is not all. The people of Puntland have shown a core of resilience. They have pulled up their bootstraps and made a previously neglected area a vibrant economy and a good place in Somalia."

Before I became prime minister, in 2010, the health minister had sent a group email to an online forum called Raswadaag, in which he talked about the plight of the Galkayo hospital. The hospital was important; it serviced nearly 800,000 people. The health minister did not get a positive response to his email, so I decided to solicit funding from the group. I began with my own contribution of $1,000. After many discussions, I was happy to note that about $14,000 had been collected for the project. This is not small change in Somalia, so it was a significant accomplishment.

In late 2010 and early 2011, when I was minister of planning and international cooperation, we received €3 million from the Spanish government. With the help of the minister of public works, Abdirashid Khalif Hashi, we agreed to use this money for social services, roads, hospitals, and so on. Approximately $403,000 of that funding was allocated to the rehabilitation of the Galkayo hospital. It was placed in a PricewaterhouseCoopers account in Nairobi when I left office.

On June 21, 2011, I had received an email from the former Italian ambassador to Somalia, Stefano Dejak, stating that Italy had funding available to provide a state-run shortwave radio and TV station for Somalia. He asked where the funds would most usefully be spent. Since Mogadishu already had the famous Radio Mogadishu and a national TV station, the next feasible option was Puntland—al-Shabaab had a stranglehold on the rest of the country—so I recommended Puntland. The TFG provided other development aid to Puntland as well, including road construction equipment, which was handed over on December 7, 2011, by the state minister of transport, Said Qorsheel, and the assistant minister of public works, Hared Hassan Ali.

In my time as prime minister, the TFG channeled a handful of development projects to Puntland. On September 21, 2011, I had a meeting with the foreign minister of Italy, Franco Frattini, and as a result Italy donated €15 million for Somalia. I decided that money should be used mainly for health and infrastructure development: €4.8 million was earmarked for health, €7 million for infrastructure, and €3.2 million for contingency. Part of the €10.2 million for infrastructure and contingency was allocated for the rebuilding of airports in Galkayo, Bosaso, Beletweyne, and Jowhar. Puntland received its share of these development projects, and the UN Office of Project Services (UNOPS) was given the contract to implement them.

I asked the Turkish ambassador to consider Somaliland and Puntland for some development projects as well, and he paid a visit to Puntland and Somaliland in April 2012. Unfortunately, on the eve of the Istanbul conference President Farole accused the Turkish government of inviting radicals and al-Shabaab. This of course was offensive to the Turkish government, and from then on the relationship between Turkey and Puntland deteriorated.

THE WAY AHEAD:

A VISION OF PROGRESS

As I look back on my experiences as minister and prime minister of Somalia the following thoughts come to mind.

When I was elected prime minister of Somalia, I saw the problems confronting the nation and realized I faced a daunting task. There was no security: al-Shabaab was positioned less than a kilometer from Villa Somalia, Somalia's resources were stretched to the limit, and the country was broken. There was extreme mistrust among Somalis, and the relationship between the TFG, the federal states, and other stakeholders and political entities had hit rock bottom. Somalia had no institutions or framework that could take the country forward.

I decided to bring people together for the good of the country. We could only achieve something if Somalis were united in purpose; the fragmentation of society was such that no meaningful work could be done without bringing people together. I brought various stakeholders to the table to deliberate. What is good for the whole is good for the parts; if the center is ailing, there is nothing the parts can do. It is a case of either mutually assured success or mutually assured destruction.

Although I brought my home region, Puntland, on board, the leaders in Southern Somalia and Puntland were not on speaking terms at that time. I was juggling the interests of various personalities and slowly trying to open the lines of communication between them. Whatever the relationship or situation, the lines of communication are fundamental—in politics, once those are closed, you are done.

There were no substantive differences between the two presidents, Farole and Sheikh Sharif; there were no disagreements on policy; there was simply discontent and discord. Farole had a sense of self-importance, and Sheikh Sharif was suffering from an inferiority complex. It was the same—self-importance—with Caalin, the president of Galmudug, who also had problems with the central government of Somalia.

I saw my task as bringing the pieces of the nation together, because I believed that as long as we were divided and disconnected nothing would move forward. It was not simply a matter of bringing the various parties to the table; it was about maintaining dialogue. It is not enough to steer the ship, you must also ensure that it moves forward.

There were times when I felt nothing could be done. Murphy's Law seemed to apply—everything that could go wrong, did go wrong. In Somalia, everything is delicate and fragile and must be handled with care; things fall apart easily. Muslims, though, are taught to persevere, to learn from mistakes and move forward. Every challenge comes with opportunity. We had to move forward, to learn from our failures, and acquire a perspective that would help us heal a broken country.

The drought of 2011 was the worst in the past 60 years. It was harrowing and humbling to see our people dying in the hundreds and thousands, and feeling there was nothing I could do. With the challenge and misery of that famine, however, came one of Somalia's greatest opportunities: the arrival of the Turkish prime minister. I wouldn't say the drought was a blessing in disguise, but as the Qur'an says, "With every trial and tribulation come blessings."

As a result of the drought and the famine, Somalia became the focus of the international community's attention. I believe that this disaster was woven with our own hands. Somalis destroyed their environment, and its protection should become a priority for every Somali government from now on. Every policy should be accompanied by an environmental impact assessment. It was tragic that a semi-arid country would be exporting millions of sacks of charcoal for the entertainment of few rich men living in foreign countries. If something were not done to reverse the trend of environmental destruction, it would have been the cause of a greater disaster in which the environment and the people would have died together. We did something during our time: with the help of James Swan, we succeeded in making the import and export of charcoal from Somalia illegal.

I gained experience and learned from my time in office that Somalis can only rely on themselves. Some members of the international community involved in Somalia were heartless and indifferent in the face of our disaster. They were unmoved by the drought enveloping the country—they didn't care. Thus it is imperative that anything we do as Somalis should be centered on local initiatives. A Somali problem is first and foremost a problem for Somalis to solve. We must take the lead; waiting for the world to help will not take us anywhere.

Another severe issue was security. In order to do any meaningful work we needed breathing space, and we knew that if we kept using the previous strategies we could not expect a different result. We tried to understand the enemy—What was their strategy? What was their MO? What was their level of force? What were their capabilities?

Al-Shabaab was a mobile force; its members would hit hard and move on, terrorizing local populations. Our counter-offensive strategy bore fruit quickly, and al-Shabaab left Mogadishu on August 6, 2011. It was becoming a spent force, and a domino effect took place in which it then lost control of the major population centers in southern Somalia. Our government then needed to continue fighting with a credible force, and we made two decisions. First, we had to negotiate with those who were willing to defect from al-Shabaab and lay down their arms. Second, we had to ensure that we fought to the end against those who were hell-bent on destroying Somalia and making it a breeding ground for violence and instability.

We could fight and defeat al-Shabaab militarily, but we also had to fight it ideologically; its ideology was abhorrent but still successful in recruiting youth to its cause. Somalis are susceptible to religious indoctrination, so we had to take advantage of the existence of moderate religious scholars to change the narrative. We wanted to make clear, especially to young people, that al-Shabaab's violent ideology is not condoned in Islam: killing people willy-nilly, stoning people to death, and similar harsh, draconian measures are not actions that the religion allows.

When I became prime minister, Somalia had been in transition for nearly twelve years, with no end in sight, and the government had to create and implement a mechanism for completion. We signed the Roadmap in September 2011 in Mogadishu. This was a framework that constrained politicians with timelines and benchmarks—it was driving us; we had to meet deadlines and complete the benchmarks. The Roadmap gave us the structure we needed; it gave us direction, and the particular importance of the Roadmap was that it accounted for the change of governance and the new political dispensation that took effect in August 2012.

There had been a draft constitution in the making for six years, and I am told that $50 million had been spent on it. After all the time and resources they had invested, many of those involved were not interested in bringing the process to a conclusion. For this reason, we decided to appoint a new group, a committee of experts to work on the constitution and speed up the process. They did a fine job, and today Somalia has a constitution, albeit a provisional one. The nation needs to hold a referendum as soon as possible.

It is very important that the new constitution of Somalia be predicated on the notion of federalism. Federalism is the only law in the land. Some Somalis, including some of the current leadership, don't support this concept and are even adamantly opposed to it, but it is not our personal opinions that matter here. Regardless of one's position in the government, the contract agreed upon included federal states. Not honoring that contract will create a crisis of confidence among the stakeholders.

Federalism can be a vehicle to bring those who are advocating or claiming secession, such as Somaliland, back into the fold. Somalia could bring them on board with a more liberal version of the Roadmap, a sort of "devolution plus," and more autonomy than the current constitution allows. We need to teach Somalis more about federalism: both those who support it and those who oppose it do so ignorantly. Centralized power has failed us: there was a time when Mogadishu was Somalia, and Somalia was Mogadishu; when Mogadishu fell, every other city did too. Mogadishu was the center, and when it broke the whole country broke. We must not return to that state of affairs.

The priority for the current government of Somalia is to continue liberating the country from al-Shabaab. The newly liberated areas need to be stabilized. Reconciliation efforts and communication

Prime Minister Abdiweli Mohamed Ali Welcome Ceremony with Prime Minister of Kuwait Jaber Al-Mubarak Al-Hamad Al-Sabah, December 5, 2011 Kuwait City,

Prime Minister David Cameron (R) gestures to Prime Minister of the Federal Government of Somalia Abdiweli Mohamed Ali during a press conference at The Foreign and Commonwealth Office on February 23, 2012 London, England

*Prime Minister Abdiweli Mohamed Ali and Italian Prime Minister
Mario Monti February 1 2012 Rome*

*Sheikh Sharif Sheikh Ahmed (right), President of Somalia, and
the country's Prime Minister, Abdiweli Mohamed Ali (left), attend
a ceremony at Mogadishu International Airport March 25, 2012
Mogadishu, Somalia UN Photo/Stuart Price*

Somalia's Prime Minister Abdiweli Mohamed Ali (L) and Kenyan Prime Minister Raila Odinga exchange the signed cooperative agreements October 31, 2011 Nairobi

among Somalis must begin in earnest. Federal states need to be established, and Jubbaland s the first test case. It is the first state to be created under the transition, and it should be supported. Other

APPENDIX

A

emerging states should also be helped and given incentives to federate.

Somalia should work hard on the delivery of humanitarian and social services to those who have suffered for the past twenty years. We need to show a government that is a better alternative than al-Shabaab,. Furthermore, a census must be taken once the country has been pacified and administrations have been established. When completed, the census must be followed by a referendum on the constitution.

In August 2016, we need to ensure free and fair elections in which one person has one vote. There is ample time between now and then to do this, and much can be done, so long as there is commitment, vision, and determination. We must look beyond personal and parochial interests. Politicians are always self-interested; yet that self-interest must accompany their realization and promotion of the public interest.

When we pursue self-interest, we might or might not achieve our goals; but if we pursue the public interest, some kind of self-interest will also be achieved. If we neglect the public interest, we cannot reach our private interest.

APPENDICES

Excerpt of Remarks to the United Nations Security Council, New York, USA, September 14, 2011

Mr. President, distinguished ambassadors, it is an honor for me to be here before you today and to update you on the developments that have occurred in Somalia. This is the first time I have had the opportunity to address the UN Security Council since my appointment as Prime Minister in June 2011. In the intervening period, the humanitarian, security and political landscape has changed and it is my intention to demonstrate the steps that the Transitional Federal Government is taking to address the new challenges and opportunities that face us today.

A month and half after my appointment as Prime Minister, Al Qaeda–affiliated extremist insurgents were forced to withdraw from the capital under pressure from the Somali National Army and with the support of the African Union Mission in Somalia. On August 10, 2011, the Special Representative of the Secretary General, Dr. Augustine Mahiga, updated the Council on the situation in the capital following this withdrawal by al Shabaab, noting that this presented both opportunities and challenges for the Transitional Federal Government as we strive to consolidate security in the city, provide public services to the population, and tackle the enormous humanitarian emergency enveloping our country.

We in Somalia recognize, as the Secretary-General's report states, that failure to deliver would fatally undermine the legitimacy and the popular support the government currently enjoys. However, we must remain realistic as we enter this next phase of our journey of saving Somalia. Stabilizing security inside the capital has been a determined focus of my government over the past month and the plan for Mogadishu is starting to work. We cannot, however, afford to be complacent. We are cognizant of the fact that pockets of insurgents remain in the city and are intent on launching a campaign of terror against the population using suicide attacks and improvised explosive devices. Already, our security and intelligence agencies have foiled a number of such attacks. And at the same time, it will be imperative to ensure that the Somali state is able to keep clan rivalries and warlordism at bay. It is essential that we work together to enlarge and improve the Somali National Army and Police. This is a matter of grave urgency. In order to consolidate and build on the security gains it is essential to enlarge the AMISOM force that has sacrificed so much and worked so hard, in the near future with the required air and maritime force components that it badly needs. To support this united effort I look forward to announcing the National Security and Stabilization Plan—a key part of the Roadmap—in the near future.

As the world marks the ten-year anniversary of the 9/11 attacks here in New York and in Washington D.C., it is critical that we learn the lessons of the past. The struggle to stabilize Somalia and deny terrorists a foothold in the Horn of Africa is one in which we all have a stake and therefore one in which we all have responsibilities. At this juncture I would like to thank the Council for the generous support it has given to both the Transitional Federal Institutions and to the AMISOM peace support mission, without whose assistance much of the progress that I have outlined above would not have been possible. In this regard, I ask the Council to urgently reconsider the recommendations of the AU Peace and Security Council to increase the mandated strength of the AMISOM force to 20,000 troops from the current ceiling of 12,000, and to provide it with key enablers and force multipliers, including air and marine components.

On the humanitarian front, as you are aware, the UN has declared famine in six regions of Somalia and half the population, or 4 million people, are now facing the prospect of starvation. Many of these continue to come to the capital seeking refuge. The UN estimated that over half a million have already arrived. A Disaster Management Agency, comprising members of civil society, has been established and we are working with UN agencies including the Office for the Coordination of Humanitarian Affairs, the UN High Commissioner for Refugees and the World Food Programme to coordinate our efforts to deal with the famine.

On behalf of the entire Somali nation, I wish to express my gratitude for the pledges of assistance that we have received from governments and humanitarian agencies around the world. It is with a matter of urgency that we seek to coordinate better and upscale the humanitarian relief. There can be no competition—only concerted effort—in a humanitarian crisis of this scale between our traditional and non-traditional donors. All estimates predict that the crisis will deepen in the country and the suffering of my kinsfolk will worsen. The greatest need, however, continues to be felt within areas still under the effective control of the extremists, where access by international humanitarian agencies is severely restricted. It is therefore critical that we accelerate efforts to reach those in al Shabaab controlled areas before the crisis spirals out of control, threatening the security and political gains made thus far. The international community must urgently reinforce our efforts to extend the zone of safety for aid workers beyond Mogadishu and into these areas.

I now turn to our political progress. In May, we informed the Council of our intention, together with the UN Political Office for Somalia, to hold a consultative meeting in Mogadishu with the aim of generating a consensus on how to bring the transition process to a successful conclusion. At the time, there existed critical disagreements between the transitional institutions on how this was to be achieved. However, with the generous help of both the Secretary-General's Special Representative for Somalia, Dr. Mahiga, and the President of Uganda, His Excellency Yoweri Museveni, we were able to bridge the gaps and come to a common agreement on the way forward in the form of the Kampala Accord. As a result, it is today my privilege to report that the Consultative Meeting on Ending the Transition was successfully held in the capital just over a week ago and concluded with the adoption of a Roadmap, complete with specific timelines and benchmarks, to ensure the return of permanent governance in August next year. Critically, my government is committed to implementing the Roadmap and delivering the priority tasks of security, the constitution, reconciliation, and good governance by August 20, 2012. In the run up to the Conference, President Sheikh Sharif and I visited Puntland and Galmudug and these visits have created a strong foundation for good working relations between the Federal Government and Regional Administrations. We have signed an agreement with the President of Puntland, which will help us further develop the relationship. Additional steps to enhance reconciliation efforts, at the national, regional and local levels, will be taken in the coming months.

Today, Somalia faces two alternative futures. One is where the humanitarian relief effort is stepped up, the international peace support force of AMISOM grows and can support the Somali Police and Army in building on the security gains made so far. At the same time, this enables the political journey to be taken to revitalize and strengthen the Somali state. The alternative, however, spells dire consequences for the state. Worsening famine with epidemics of cholera and measles; destroying the country's social fabric and ruining economic livelihoods for a generation. All the while,

seriously overstretched TFG and AMISOM forces are unable to stop al Shabaab regrouping. Allied with the enemies of peace in Somalia, they attack the fragile security in the capital and fatally undermine all efforts to re-build Somalia.

A week ago I signed the Roadmap, on behalf of the TFG and in cooperation with the Transitional Federal Parliament, the Puntland State of Somalia, Galmudug, Ahlu Sunna Wal Jama'a, I am confident we can lead Somalia towards growing social, economic and political stability. However, Somalia's future hangs in the balance and so we cannot take this journey alone. As I stand here today and pledge my commitment to delivering the priority tasks laid out in the Roadmap so I ask the international support necessary to deliver the humanitarian relief and security that are vital components of stabilizing Somalia.

Let me conclude by saying that while efforts to ameliorate the effects of famine will continue to demand our attention in the short term, we will not lose sight of the fact that the progress made on the security and political fronts is laying the foundation for a secure Somali state, representative of and capable of delivering to its own people. With the increased and concerted commitment of the international community, I am confident that Somalia will overcome present difficulties and take the path towards peace and stability.

Excerpts of Speech to the United Nations General Assembly, New York, USA, September 24, 2011

Mr. President, Mr. Secretary-General, fellow delegates, ladies and gentlemen, it is a great pleasure to address this august group of participants here today. Mr. President, let me take this opportunity to congratulate you on your election as President of the Sixty-Sixth Session of the United Nations General Assembly. I would also like to congratulate our Secretary General of the United Nations on his re-election for a second term. We Somalis would like to thank him for his leadership as he put Somalia on the top of the agenda despite having too many competing priorities. We hope that Somalia will become peaceful and stable during his tenure.

It is my honor to address you for the first time as the Prime Minister of Somalia. I come before you mindful of the enormous challenges of this important moment in our history and determined to act boldly in the cause of peace, justice and stability, not only in the Horn of Africa but on the African continent at large and in the world as a whole.

The seemingly unending humanitarian crisis in Somalia has many and varied causes including decades of conflict, the demise of the central state, poor and kleptocratic leadership, and struggles between clans for limited resources, exacerbated by cycles of devastating droughts. This has created chronic food shortages, an underdeveloped economy, and has driven the population to despair. In recent years, the global terrorist organization, Al Qaeda, has sought to exploit these divisions and weaknesses to plot and execute attacks on the rest of the world. Our people know only too well the destruction that a few people, blinded by an ideology of extremism and terror, can wreak on a country. It is this small minority, primarily the Al Qaeda–affiliated group al Shabaab, that is responsible for the current famine that is spreading throughout the country through their polices of systematically looting grain stores; forcible recruitment of and extortion from farmers and their families; and preventing aid agencies access to the most affected regions in the country. However, the threat they pose is not limited to our borders. Foreign fighters have sought to export their noxious extremism to the rest of the Horn, recruiting and sponsoring acts of terror in neighboring countries such as Uganda, where last year they murdered 76 innocent people. The insecurity they have created in the south of Somalia has led to a large influx of refugees into Kenya and Ethiopia, straining resources and spreading instability across the region.

They are actively planning to strike further afield. Just this week, one of the leaders of al Shabaab said the group is committed to continuing its battle against the government of Somalia and also seeks to destroy both the United States and the United Nations. It is also a well-known fact that al Shabaab has been focusing their recruitment and radicalization efforts on the Somali Diaspora in Australia, Europe, Canada and in the USA.

Clearly, the battle against Al Qaeda is one in which we all have a stake and in which we all, therefore, have responsibilities. In Somalia, we have been doing what we can, within our limited resources, to fulfill our obligations in this regard.

Somalia's leaders are redoubling efforts to achieve national reconciliation and entrench democratic governance. Three weeks ago, with the help of our international partners, we hosted a National Consultative Conference in Mogadishu—the first—during which the transitional institutions and representatives of regional administrations came together to adopt a Roadmap to the re-establishment of permanent, legitimate and representative government for the country.

Going forward, as we embark on the final leg of the transition process, we will continue to need your help and support. The Roadmap has illuminated the path and though dangers may lie in the shadows, we will not divert from it. We ask that you continue to accompany us on this journey and continue to provide needed resources as we advance towards full sovereignty.

The effort must begin at home. Let me be the first to acknowledge that, in the past, we Somalis made mistakes, which eroded the trust the international community has in our institutions. Somalia can and must do better. In this time of national crisis, we the Somali people must set aside our differences and come together to confront the perils. Reconciliation must become our mantra as we work to further the peace process and create an environment conducive

APPENDIX C

for the delivery of aid. We in the political class must also accept our responsibility for the errors of the past and must be resolute to do better. The Somali people have had enough of war and hunger; enough of political wrangling and corruption. They demand, and indeed deserve, a government that puts the national interest before personal ambition; one that fosters unity, not division.

To the business community, I say Somalia is truly Africa's sleeping giant and a relatively small investment here will go a long way. With the longest coastline on the continent, bountiful and unexploited natural wealth and an entrepreneurial tradition that dates back to the Roman times, a peaceful Somalia would be a force for moderation and an engine of growth and prosperity for the region and for the continent. Further, the integration of Somalia into the global economy will have a considerable and beneficial impact on the phenomenon of piracy on our shores, which imposes huge costs on global trade.

In conclusion, today the future of Somalia hangs in the balance and with it the prospect of peace, stability and prosperity on the Horn of Africa and security for nations across the world. Resolute global action in support of our efforts is now required if we are to consolidate and build on the gains already made, and extend them to the rest of the country for the sake of future generations.

Opening Remarks at the Garowe 1 Conference, Garowe, Puntland, Somalia, December 2011

Mr. President, Mr. Speaker, President Farole, President Caalim, Ministers, parliamentarians, other functionaries in our government,

Ambassador Mahiga, our friends from the international community, the people of Puntland and most particularly residents of Garowe, greetings.

I am very honored to take part in this historic event and especially in the city of Garowe, Puntland. Let me explain first on the importance of this conference. You would all recall that my government together with our stakeholder partners made a commitment to end the permanent transition that we have condemned ourselves to for the last 20 years. Imagine a transition that lasts 21 years. You will agree that a permanent transition is an oxymoron, a contradiction in terms. A transition must have proscribed beginning date and an end date and the term ought to be short in duration. Not in our case.

Everything in our lives has been and continues to be in a transition. Our lives are in transitions of refuge, civil wars, human displacements and human rights violations. Our children, those in refugee camps and those in exile are in transitions. The largest and most permanent refugee camp in the world is Dhadhaab; a camp started as a transitional camp in 1991 and now has become a metropolitan city known entirely for its abject poverty and inhumane conditions. Our governance structures have been in flux and in state of transition for 21 years and this government I am leading is also a transitional government.

To me this conference represents the possibility of a new beginning, the possibility for the Somali people to say "ENOUGH" to transitions, transitions of the personal kind and those of governance institutions. I appeal to all of you to put your heads together in the next few days and come up with creative models of ending this permanent transition.

A society that is in endless transitions cannot plan for a sustainable future, cannot have a national economic planning regime, cannot aim to provide acceptable levels of services for society, and cannot aspire for a peaceful community that is at ease with itself and at peace with its neighbors. We must end this transition and the means to end is clearly provided for in the Roadmap, an agreement that we all committed to in September 2011 in Mogadishu. The Roadmap directs us to undertake the following: We must complete the constitution in a timely fashion, we must all engage in reconciliation and political outreach; we are in the middle of fashioning integrity institutions that can better guide us into good governance regime that is on par with international standards and lastly, we must secure the country from extremism.

Let me also remind our partners that we cannot do all of these

things on our own and that we need assistance. As a matter of fact, when we were preparing the Roadmap benchmarks and timelines, you also committed that you would provide us with the required resources to implement the Roadmap tasks. As my government reminded you time and again, we are waiting for a genuine commitment on your part to commit the resources while we commit to the process.

Let me also remind you that time is of the essence. To move forward, the Somali people require of you to bring forth key principles that can end this transition, principles that are process driven, are fair and forward looking.

Garowe is also symbolically important to me. Here is why: A few years ago, I began volunteering at this very university (Puntland State University) during my summer vacations and today the same university is hosting a national agenda of which I am an important part. It is historic for me on a personal level; it is also historic for the students I taught in here. I also hope that it will be historic for one more reason of national importance. If we collectively produce some key and guiding principles on ending this ugly transition, these principles would no doubt be called the "Garowe Principles," an accolade that will forever be etched in Somali history.

Remarks at the London Conference, London, England, February 2012

Ladies and gentlemen, I thank you for the opportunity to speak before you here. My vision is a secure, stable and prosperous Somalia; a Somalia at peace with itself and with its neighbors, where its citizens can go about their daily lives in safety and provide for their families with confidence and dignity. A resurgent, tolerant Somali society where conflicts are resolved peacefully, built on respect for traditional Somali culture, religious values and way of life. A Somalia with an inclusive and accountable system of government that represents all of its people and in which all Somalis can feel they have a stake. Achieving this of course represents a huge challenge. But it is not a Utopian dream, it can be done and we are closer than many people think.

Somalia's problems are long standing and complicated. Solving them requires a serious and honest partnership between the Transitional Institutions, the African Union, the United Nations and the broader International Community.

I can tell you that we now have a genuine window of opportunity for Somalis to achieve the vision that I have just described ... The foremost challenge we therefore face today in Somalia is to rebuild the institutions that enable community; to end the anarchy of statelessness and introduce a new order built on the bonds of language, culture, and religion that unite us.

An ancient Somali proverb promises that if people come together, they can even mend a crack in the sky. And today we are witnessing the humble beginnings of a drive by the Somali people to take their destiny into their own hands and to shape their future. We are under no illusions about the skepticism in which this proposition attracts among both the Somali people and the international community. Two decades of seemingly unending humanitarian crisis, and inept and kleptocratic leadership have driven many to despair.

We Somalis are stubbornly independent-minded. One 19th century visitor noted that it was a land where every man was his own Sultan. This can be the source of enduring strength. But it has in more recent times been exploited by the selfish and the greedy to divide the people.

Greedy individuals have manipulated clan affiliations, fractured the national identity and turned the levers of state into the instruments of self-enrichment. We must now remodel these institutions to become the tools that rejuvenate the national consciousness that arises out of our common heritage.

The Political Roadmap we adopted in Mogadishu last year

was the culmination of Somali-led reconciliation initiatives, dating back to the Arta Declaration of May 2000 which established the Transitional National Government. Over the course of more than a decade, the transition process has expanded to include many who had initially opposed it. In 2003, the TNG merged with the rival Somalia Reconciliation and Restoration Council to form the Transitional Federal Government. Other factions have since been incorporated into the TFG, including the moderate wing of the Islamic Courts Union in 2008 and the Ahlu Sunna Wal Jamaa two years later. It is therefore clear that while the process has not always been smooth, it has nonetheless proven to be inclusive, locally driven and something that all Somalis can rightly take pride in. However, Garowe has now shown that it is time to return both the process and the country to their rightful owners: the people of Somalia. And, come August, so it will be.

There must be no further extension of the transition. With the help of our neighbors and friends on the African continent and beyond, we are making progress on the four strategic goals of the Roadmap: security; reconciliation and political outreach; completion of the constitution-making process; and delivery of good governance.

As different parts of the country are liberated from the insurgents, the Transitional Federal Government will need to take a leading role in establishing peace, fostering reconciliation and establishing the structures for democratic, accountable and efficient local and regional governance. We have therefore developed a 3-year National Stabilization and Security Plan that is hinged on the continuing work to rebuild the national army, police force and institutions of justice.

The disarmament, demobilization and reintegration into society of those defecting from the extremist groups will be critical.

APPENDIX E

After twenty years of continuous conflict, the country is literally overflowing with arms and many young people have not known peace throughout their lifetime.

The endless anarchy and resultant grinding poverty has robbed them of hope. Restoring their faith in society and reintegrating them back into their communities is a long-term task that must begin now. We must devise means to welcome and assist the rising numbers of defectors from the extremists' ranks.

We must also find effective means to counter the soul-destroying radicalization and extremism that is being spread by Al Qaeda, not just in Somalia but in Somali communities around the world. This is absolutely critical if we are to secure the future.

Peace, stability and economic progress in Somalia are in all our interests. Terrorism, piracy, famine and displacement are all symptoms and not causes of Somalia's problems. Good and legitimate government that is relevant and trusted by the people of Somalia, within effective security architecture under the rule of law is the answer. This, therefore, is the task we have set for ourselves. It is unspeakably ambitious and the path is full of potential pitfalls. But fortune favors the brave and the long-suffering people of Somalia deserve no less. We have set our hand to the task and will not turn back.

Opening Statement at the Istanbul Conference, Istanbul, Turkey, May 31, 2012

Excellencies, distinguished participants, ladies and gentlemen, Somalia and Turkey have profound historical relations dating back to the Middle Ages and the ties between the Adal Sultanate and the Ottoman Empire going back to the 16th Century, during the Ottoman Empire and the rule of Sultan Salim I in 1517. Turkey has recently revived this relationship in a very unique way and the people of Somalia are forever indebted to Turkey to reaching out in a time of need.

[...] My goal is to bring stability that will lead to the Somali people taking charge of their country. We need to guide Somalia towards a new direction, a fresh start, away from labels such as "the world's worst failed state"—back to the proud independent nation we've always been, a nation of autonomous, vital, self-reliant men and women, the nation of poets, respected in this part of the world for nearly a millennium.

Somalia is more than hungry faces in the news, pirates or extremists; it is a diverse, rich land with historical pedigree. I can foresee a day where Somalia has an active, vibrant economy buoyed by modern infrastructure and by highways, a Somalia with a highly educated young professional class, a Somalia where one can travel in peace in the dead of the night, a Somalia where we play an essential part of an "East African Economic zone," with trade booming across this region, fuelling the global economy. A Somalia with an export-led economy rather than an import-fuelled economy. A Somalia that is a business hub, connecting Asia and Africa. A Somalia where our society is fed by a rich cultural life. This is what I think Somalia can and will be—Inshallah.

[...] Our challenge as Somalis is how to tap into this great wealth and use it to bring our country and our people back onto the global economic playing field, which brings us to this conference. I would like to point out three ideas that I want you all to keep in mind over the next two days:

- First, Somalia's future is in the hands of Somalis. Only we can shift our path towards prosperity and peace, and we can achieve this only by engaging with each other and rolling up our sleeves. The last few days in Istanbul have provided us with another platform to have this exchange and we are grateful to the Turkish government.

- Second, as we pursue Somali-led solutions, we need the international community to unite behind our vision. This conference will be successful if the international community succeeds in adopting a common position on the future of Somalia. Turkey's active presence in Somalia has provided a tangible example of a new development paradigm. I hope the rest of our partners draw useful parallels from Turkey's example.

- Third, we need to think long term. Somalia is ready for development. If we do not work on longer-term development, we will always be faced with short-term crisis management.

[…] As we move forward into the new Somalia, our focus must be on the "four modernizations":

1. Security

2. Economy

3. Agriculture and livestock

4. Scientific and technological development

These themes will be explored further in the next two days. Given the destruction of the last 20 years, Somalia requires a huge reconstruction and development plan, and a correspondingly huge infusion of resources. These resources will come from Somali entrepreneurship

APPENDIX

F

fused with strategic partnerships. We will rely on the human capital of returning Somali professionals as well as training our people back home. If I may quote a famous line, "education is the passport to the future for tomorrow belongs to those who prepare for it today." We call for strategic trade relationships, and foreign direct investment in Somalia. We call for a multilateral trust fund for Somalia, to be focused on reconstruction and development. The need is too great for one donor to manage, so we are asking for multiple donors to set up a trust fund.

Ladies and Gentlemen, Somalia's on the verge of a new dawn. We must be ready to seize the moment and build on the foundations we've laid this past year. We owe it to our children and their children to give them a better future. Today Mogadishu is thriving as a result of the security gains of the past 9 months thanks to the TFG Forces, AMISOM and neighboring countries, as well as the Turkish direct investments in infrastructure, construction and social services. This is the model for the country as we look to the future—security plus investment.

Excellencies, distinguished participants, ladies and gentlemen, I am optimistic about the possibilities for Somalia and I hope you share my enthusiasm. I thank you for your active participation at this conference, and for your contributions to the people of Somalia.

Remarks to the United Nations General Assembly, New York, USA, September 20, 2012

[…] Just over two weeks ago, Somalia took a bold and decisive step away from decades of division, disorder and conflict, and instead towards the reconstitution of a more representative, more democratic Somali republic at peace with itself, with its neighbors and with the rest of the world.

[…] For more than two decades of crisis, the Somali people have suffered and endured, but we have not done so alone. The United Nations have stood by us, providing humanitarian assistance to those of our people in need, helping us to rebuild from the ruins of war, bringing us time and again to the negotiating table to resolve our differences, and maintaining the dignity of the Somali nation by keeping our flag flying through these long, dark years … Somalia's progress is also due in great measure to the selfless courage and sacrifice of our brothers and sisters in the African Union, including our closest neighbors, whose forces have fought long and hard, with so many laying down their lives in the battle to give our children a better future … We thank our international partners who are diligently supporting AMISOM, especially the European Union and the US amongst others … The members of the League of Arab States and the Organization of Islamic Conference have also extended the hand of friendship to the Somali people during these difficult times. We are especially grateful to the government and people of Turkey, for their faith, courage and leadership in ending our long isolation, and building bridges between Somalia and the rest of the world.

But now, with all these partners standing by us we must increasingly learn to travel our own path with our own energies, developing the ability to stand on our own feet, and step free from the reliance of our kind friends. Already, the Somali diaspora from around the world are returning to the country with investment and skills that will build the future Somalia. We can learn from how peace and growing prosperity has developed in other parts of the country. We must build on the return of normality in Mogadishu, and elsewhere in Somalia, and growing public confidence in the future. It is the Somali people, in the villages and the nomadic pastoralists, with their resilience, drive and dynamism that are best placed to lend real stability to Somalia's future.

[…] Somalia's transition has officially ended, but the work of rebuilding our nation continues. The new administration has four short years to translate agreements and objectives made on paper into concrete, tangible progress for our people, and to place Somalia firmly on an irreversible path to enduring peace and growing prosperity. The most urgent challenge is to restore peace and security throughout Somali territory. Our forces, together with our African Union allies, are making great progress in this regard. But a stable peace cannot be achieved through military means alone. We must practice the politics of inclusion, establishing a credible, representative, inclusive and capable government: a government by the people, for the people; not government of the few, serving the interests of the few. Initially that government must be about delivering real governance and connections with the people; it must be about the process of building local representation, addressing community justice and seeking to build basic services, rather than about distant institutions of government from Mogadishu, or even provincial centers.

Power and responsibility must be devolved as close to the people as possible in accordance with the principles of federalism. It will be important to recognize the existence of other Somali authorities, as well as de facto political and military forces across the country, with whom we will work to establish a vibrant, prosperous and stable representative government democracy, firmly adhering to and grounded in Somali and Islamic values. And we will require a fair and independent judiciary, resistant to executive interference, which will meet the needs and earn the trust of ordinary citizens, while bringing an end to the culture of impunity that has gripped our nation for the past two decades.

[...] We Somalis have a saying: Colaad kasta nabad baa ka dambeysa—"After every war comes peace." So let us remember that we have no choice as a nation but to live together; let us settle our differences through dialogue and compromise, so that there is no longer any justification for any Somali to take up arms against another.

[...] The road ahead is long, but we the Somali people are committed and we are ready. We have created the guideposts, and we have chosen a new leadership to help us move forward. We are grateful for the support of the world community—we would not be here today without your moral, political and financial support. Most dear to us is the personal sacrifices made by our African brothers and sisters who have come in person to help us protect our country and people. We cannot thank you enough and we hope one day to be able to repay you.

As many today have noted, the United Nations was founded on the conviction that the nations of the world could come together in the spirit of cooperation to tackle their common problems for the sake of the whole of humanity.

The world is going through a challenging period—economic crises, religious tensions, resource disputes. Every nation has its own challenges and priorities. And yet, we come together as the United Nations to forge a common way forward because we recognize that this small earth is all the space we have and we must find a way to share it and coexist peacefully.

As Somalis, we have learned this hard lesson through bitter experience, and we are living through it every day, each time another young man chooses to take his own life and the lives of others; each time a young mother has to bury a child. Let us not forget that in rebuilding a nation, or in steering the world to a better place, we are dealing with the lives of human beings, each life as precious as the next. For the future of our children, we must work harder to make our world peaceful and prosperous.

[…] The Members of this Assembly are no strangers to conflict and war. Many countries have experienced violence and destruction equal to or greater than my own. But few other countries in modern times have experienced such a prolonged period of "statelessness": a nation without a recognized government, a valid passport or a convertible currency. But it is not just the material attributes of statehood that we have missed. To be "stateless" in this world of States is injurious to a people's identity, to its rights and privileges as a nation, and to its dignity.

It is time for us to reclaim Somalia's rightful place in the community of nations, to shoulder our duties and obligations, and to place our country in the service of peace, security and prosperity of this planet we share. On my behalf and on behalf of the people of Somalia and our H.E. President Hassan Sheikh Mohamud, I thank you.